# The Mountains
# in Art History

# The Mountains in Art History

*Edited by Peter Mark*
*Peter Helman and Penny Snyder*

Wesleyan University Press | Middletown, Connecticut

Wesleyan University Press

Middletown, CT 06459

www.wesleyan.edu/wespress

2017 © Wesleyan University

All rights reserved

Manufactured in the United States of America

5 4 3 2 1

Library of Congress Cataloging-in-Publication Data

Mark, Peter, 1948- editor.

The mountains in art history / Edited by Peter Mark ; with Peter
    Helman and Penny Snyder.

Middletown, CT : Wesleyan University Press, 2017. | Includes
    bibliographical references.

LCCN 2016049088 (print) | LCCN 2016050449 (ebook) | ISBN
    9780819577290 (pbk. : alk. paper) | ISBN 9780819577306 (ebook)

LCSH: Mountains in art--Historiography.

LCC N8213 .M697 2017 (print) | LCC N8213 (ebook) | DDC
    704.9/436143--dc23

LC record available at https://lccn.loc.gov/2016049088

# CONTENTS

# INTRODUCTION: "COMING ROUND" AGAIN

*Peter Mark*

My skis swished across the crusted snow as fog billowed over the feature-less plateau, obliterating any sense of direction. I stopped to take another compass bearing. By now, I should have completed the circuit across this Norwegian massif. Still, there was no sign of the access trail I had climbed hours before, in the half-light of a January morning. I was alone in the Jotunheimen Mountains. Suddenly, ski tracks appeared; someone else must be up here above the tree line. I followed their trail. Then, for a brief moment, the fog thinned; the entire ridge lay visible. After three hours ski-ing in whiteout, I could see. The tracks were my own.

I had come to Norway for a week in mid-winter to take a break from graduate school and to learn to cross-country ski. I would stay for three weeks. As reading matter for the long—very long—nights, I had brought Thomas Mann's *The Magic Mountain* (*Der Zauberberg*). A week after my adventure, I came to the chapter "Snow," in which Mann's protagonist, Hans Castorp, has a high-altitude epiphany. Teaching himself to cross-country ski, Castorp climbs into the Swiss Alps above Davos. He is caught in a blizzard above the forest; and in the wind and the driving snow, he loses all sense both of time and of direction. Eventually, he comes to a hut, only to realize that this had been the starting point of his storm-driven per-egrination. He has circled back on his own tracks for, as he muses, one must "come round" again. Here, in the sublime heart of the mountains in winter, Castorp proceeds to have a vision and the revelation: "I will let death have no mastery over my thoughts."[1] Indeed, the mountains, with their sublime danger, have engendered his vision of life.

For some of us, it takes rather longer "to come round." After my own ski adventure in Norway, I embarked on a career doing research in Africa and teaching art history. It has taken me 40 years to come round again. Back to the snow and to the mountains, to the sublime; to come home.

In 2007, I decided to marry my passion for hiking, climbing, and skiing to my career as an art historian. I would teach a new course about mountains as artistic inspiration and about mountain ranges (including Alpine passes) as conduits for, rather than barriers to the transmission of culture. It took me several years, first to construct a coherent course around these twin themes, and then to convince my colleagues to allow their Africanist to turn away from the heat of West Africa and to offer a course about the ice and snow. The first year, fifteen courageous Wesleyan students registered for this pedagogical experiment. Together, we learned. I can say that we taught each other. If you want to learn about a new subject, if you want to understand the unifying themes, my advice is: go teach that subject.

Gradually the themes emerged: mountain passes as highways for the exchange of artistic styles; mountains as the embodiment of the sublime. ("But what," my students still ask, "is the sublime?") The central importance of the Romantic era emerged as another theme. And we compared the artistic image of the sublime, as expressed in the paintings of Caspar David Friedrich and J.M.W. Turner, to the literary image articulated by Wordsworth, by the German writer Adalbert Stifter, and especially by the too-little-known Franz Michael Felder. I had to translate passages of his wonderful, sensitive autobiography about growing up in Austria's Bregenzerwald in the mid-nineteenth century. *Aus meinem Leben* richly deserves a full English translation.

In 2014, I taught the course again. The second group of students benefited—I hope—from an increased sense of focus; this was a byproduct of the first iteration. And like the first time around, I benefited from my students' enthusiasm and their insights. I am fortunate; I am the only person who is allowed to "take" this course more than once! But there remains one small problem: were one to teach "The Mountains and Art History" as *"Die Berge und die Kunstgeschichte"* in German, there would be a wealth of literature to read and to discuss. In English, not so much.

Together, my students and I have decided to take one small step to help improve this situation. We are making available to future students and also to a wider public, some of our own varied reflections and art historical musings about the mountains and the history of art. With the active support of Wesleyan University, we have undertaken this project: to edit and publish a collection of student essays from the first two iterations of this course. We wish you, the reader, "happy climbing."

## Notes

1. Thomas Mann, *The Magic Mountain* (New York: Modern Library, 1992), 153.

# MOUNTAINS IN ITALIAN RENAISSANCE DEPICTIONS OF "THE SACRIFICE OF ISAAC"

*Penny Snyder*

The Italian Renaissance marked a flowering in production and innovation in art. Inquiries into the nature of art itself, such as Leon Battista Alberti's treatise *De Pictura*,[1] along with such factors as competition and an interest in math and science, motivated a dedication to realism in art. This push for increased realism occasioned a growing interest in landscape in art. The natural world became a subject worth depicting as real space, rather than as an abstraction or a backdrop, as was typical of medieval art. The depiction of the natural world in art was not limited to the heightened realism of landscapes; it became a source of symbolism and meaning as well. Mountains in four different works depicting the Sacrifice of Isaac create realistic, believable spaces, but they also perform a symbolic function. Occupying a physical space between the terrestrial and the heavenly, mountains in this otherworldly space become a place of communication with God.

Mountains are the location for several important stories in the Old Testament. The revelation of the Ten Commandments to Moses and the Sacrifice of Isaac both occur on mountains, Mount Sinai and Mount Moriah respectively, establishing mountains symbolically and literally as holy places in the Bible. In both stories, mountains become a setting in which God reveals himself, either directly or through angels, to chosen humans.

In the story of the Sacrifice of Isaac, God commands Abraham to sacrifice his son on a mountain, demanding Abraham to, "Take your son, your only son, whom you love—Isaac—and go to the region of Moriah. Sacrifice him there as a burnt offering on a mountain I will show you."[2] Abraham unquestioningly follows God's directives; leaving his slaves and donkey at the foot of the mountain, he brings Isaac to the top of the mountain and binds him to an altar for slaughter. As Abraham prepares to wield the knife against his son, an angel of the Lord intervenes, stopping him. Elevated above the earthly realm, Mount Moriah becomes a space for communication with God. However, the mountain also becomes a barrier between the chosen few and the servants, who are left at the bottom of the mountain.

The revelation of the Ten Commandments shows a similar role for mountains as a place of both communication and exclusion. God calls Moses to Mount Sinai, commanding that he leave many of God's worshippers at the foot of the mountain, saying, "Go down and warn the people so they do not force their way through to see the Lord. . . . Even the priests, who approach the Lord, must consecrate themselves, or the Lord will break out against them."[3] After forty days, Moses and other chosen individuals return with the tablets. Mount Sinai is thus a bridge between the heavenly and the terrestrial, but also a barrier. In both stories, mountains serve to physically elevate specific individuals heavenward to commune with God.

The role of mountains as a space for communication in the Bible informs artistic depictions of the Sacrifice of Isaac. The competition panels for the Florence Baptistery doors (1401–1402) are among the most famous examples of the Sacrifice of Isaac in Renaissance art. While many competed for the prestigious job, the panels of Filippo Brunelleschi (1377–1446) and Lorenzo Ghiberti (1378–1455) were the forerunners, with Ghiberti ultimately winning. Brunelleschi and Ghiberti were subjected to the same constraints for the competition, such as the quatrefoil frame; but they approached the reliefs very differently, and mountains have differing levels of importance in each panel. Brunelleschi's panel (1401, bronze) is brutal and direct, focusing on the raw emotion of the event. The knife is in Abraham's hand, pressed up against Isaac's throat, who screams in terror, forcing the angel to physically intervene. The frame is divided into two by a horizontal line, between the characters participating in the action and the servants below who are unaware of the events occurring. The contradiction between the calm, oblivious characters below and the characters above serves to heighten the energy of the piece. The figures' bodies in the upper half exude energy. For example, Isaac's body is contorted in agony as his father abrasively grabs his neck. Two figures on the bottom of the panel hang over the side onto the frame; the panel is so bursting with energy that it cannot be contained within the quatrefoil frame. But while the emotions the figures display are precise, the landscape is not. Mount Moriah is abstracted into a rocky setting that functions merely as a backdrop for the work. The figures in the lower register do not interact with the landscape. The mountains in Brunelleschi's panel are downplayed in favor of the emotional intensity created by the interactions between the main figures.

While Brunelleschi focuses on the characters in the work, Ghiberti uses the landscape to suggest the violence of the sacrifice. The figures in Ghiberti's panel (1401, 1403–1424, bronze) are calm and graceful. Abraham holds the knife above Isaac's head, only requiring the angel to verbally command him to stop, unlike the physical confrontation necessary in Brunelleschi's work. The figures are less emotive; for example, Isaac is depicted as a classical nude and he seems almost proud to display his body, unlike his contortion in Brunelleschi's panel. But while the figures suggest less raw emotion, Ghiberti's work is not unemotional. Ghiberti creates a realistic setting of the craggy rocks of Mount Moriah, unlike the static backdrop in Brunelleschi's work. The lines and the texture of the rocky expanse in the middle of the work convey movement, animating the work. The jagged rocks are juxtaposed with the graceful emotions of the figures and their smooth drapery, heightening the intensity of the drama. The rocks slice the work in half, physically isolating the figures who interact with God from the servants and donkey on the left. The mountains become a literal barrier in the work, as well as a reminder that not all individuals are chosen to interact with God. The jagged rocks of Mount Moriah create intensity through line and texture, but they also create a paradoxically violent and sacred place of conversation with God.

Ghiberti returned to the Sacrifice of Isaac in another set of doors for the Florence Baptistery (1425–1452, gilded bronze). These doors, later termed by Michelangelo "The Gates of Paradise," only had ten panels, each of which was enlarged and not required to be in quatrefoil. The increased area to work with allowed Ghiberti to delve further into the landscape of Mount Moriah in his second depiction of the Sacrifice. The landscape of this sacrifice is more realistic than the previous works, with mountains in the background, a sense of elevation of Abraham and Isaac, and non-idealized flora growing in the landscape. The high relief and the angular, jutting lines of the rocks create energy in an otherwise stable piece. The narrative is spread out in three different areas of the work; Abraham meets the three angels at the bottom left, the servants and donkey wait at the foot of the mountain, and the event of the sacrifice occurs on top of the mountain. While the narrative is spatially fragmented, landscape makes the work a coherent whole, with mountains playing an important role in the interaction between Abraham and Isaac and the servants below. Ghiberti writes of "how the servants and the ass remain at the foot of the mountain, and how he has undressed Isaac and wants to sacrifice him and [how] the angel seizes the hand with the knife and shows him the ram."[4] Ghiberti notes that the servants and donkey stay at the bottom of the mountain, making mountains an isolating force between holy and secular figures. Unlike the abstracted rocks in the previous reliefs, Ghiberti depicts Mount Moriah with a sense of elevation. By being on top of the mountain, Abraham and Isaac are higher than the other figures in the work, a physical manifestation of their closeness to God. The mountains become more than just a setting in Ghiberti's panel, playing a role as a physical representation of the separation between holy and non-holy figures.

Turning from reliefs to paintings, Andrea del Sarto (1486–1530) and Caravaggio (1571–1610) both skillfully represented the Sacrifice of Isaac on canvas. Both works feature or allude to the mountainous setting of the sacrifice, but mountains in Andrea del Sarto's work play a bigger role than in Caravaggio's. In a lengthy description of Andrea del Sarto's painting (1527, oil on wood), Giorgio Vasari (1511–1574) praises the setting as "a landscape so well represented that the real scene of the event could not have been more beautiful or in any way different."[5] The small Renaissance town below gives a sense of perspective to the work, but the mountains are most important to the work. Similarly to Ghiberti's reliefs, the mountainous landscape serves to isolate Abraham, Isaac and the angel from the earthly. The three characters occupy a heavenly plane on the top of a cliff with a jagged drop-off, again suggesting the idea of mountains as a boundary between the holy and non-holy.

Unlike Andrea del Sarto's painting, Caravaggio's work (1594–6?, oil on canvas) focuses less on the landscape and more on the brutal emotions of the figures, creating intensity reminiscent of Brunelleschi's work. Caravaggio forgoes depicting extraneous parts of the story; for example, he entirely removes the donkey and servants. The figures occupy the foreground and are magnified; the angel and ram's bodies are even cut off by the frames. Because the painting focuses so intimately on the figures, it emphasizes the emotions of the characters, such as Isaac's frozen, terrified face. Caravaggio also uses chiaroscuro to heighten this emotional intensity, with vivid contrasts between the light, or holiness of the characters, and the dark of the rocks and the town below. The chiaroscuro serves to visually isolate the figures, unlike the mountains in Andrea del Sarto's work. There is a sense of elevation above the small town, and there is one rock formation to the right of Abraham's body, but these details are extraneous to the interplay between the characters. Even though Caravaggio creates a very realistic mountainous landscape, he focuses on the dramatic intensity of the work through emotions.

Mountains implicitly become sacred spaces in each of the works detailing Isaac's sacrifice by becoming the site of a holy interaction between humans and God. However, the degree to which mountains are important symbolically in each work varies; they serve as a simple backdrop in some, but as an important symbolic device in others. The works were clearly affected by artistic theories of the Renaissance as well as biblical interpretations of the sacrifice. Newfound dedication to realism in depicting the natural world played a role in Ghiberti's and Andrea del Sarto's landscapes; but so too did theories about emotions in art, especially in Brunelleschi and Caravaggio's works. Nonetheless, the majesty, intensity and mystery of the mountains are a fitting setting for such a powerful story of God's will.

# Notes

1. Leon Battista Alberti, *De Pictura* (originally *Della pittura*, 1435; *On Painting*. Penguin Classics, 1972).

2. Genesis 22.2 New International Version.

3. Exodus 19.21–42 NIV.

4. Christie Knapp Fengler, "Lorenzo Ghiberti's Second Commentary: The Translation and Interpretation of a Fundamental Renaissance Treatise on Art" (PhD diss., Graduate School of the University of Wisconsin, 1974), 66.

5. Giorgio Vasari. *Lives of the painters, sculptors and architects,* trans. Gaston du C. de Vere (New York, Random House, 1996), 849.

# Images

Lorenzo Ghiberti (1378–1455)
*Sacrifice of Isaac,* 1401–1402
gilt bronze, 21 x 17 inches
Museo nazionale del Bargello (Florence, Italy)
Wesleyan University ARTstor ID ghiberti_comp_ghib_color_01_post_srgb_8b.fpx
http://library.artstor.org.ezproxy.wesleyan.edu/library/secure/ViewImages?id=9j5B
    fzIxLCklNygnFTx5TnYqXXooeQ%3D%3D&userId=hzBH&zoomparams=

Lorenzo Ghiberti (1378–1455)
*The Gates of Paradise,* 1425–1452
individual reliefs: 31 ¼ inches square, gilded bronze
Duomo Museum of Florence
http://www.museumsinflorence.com/foto/Battistero/image/pages/isacco.html

Filippo Brunelleschi (1337–1446)
*The Sacrifice of Isaac,* 1401
bronze relief, partly gilded, 465 x 400 mm, including frame
Museo nazionale del Bargello (Florence, Italy)
Wesleyan University ARTstor ID 40-11-25/12
http://library.artstor.org.ezproxy.wesleyan.edu/library/secure/ViewImages?id=%2
    FThWdC8hIywtPygxFTx5TnQkVnwndg%3D%3D&userId=hzBH&zoomparams=

Andrea del Sarto (1486-1530)
*The Sacrifice of Isaac,* c. 1527
oil on wood, Framed: 208.00 x 171.00 x 12.50 cm (81 7/8 x 67 5/16 x 4 7/8 inches);
    Unframed: 178.00 x 138.00 cm (70 1/16 x 54 5/16 inches)

Cleveland Museum of Art, 217 Italian Baroque
https://www.clevelandart.org/art/1937.577

Michelangelo Merisi da Caravaggio (1573–1610)
*Sacrifice of Isaac*, 1594?
104 x 135 cm, oil on canvas
Galleria degli Uffizi, Florence
Wesleyan University ARTstor ID ARTSTOR_103_41822000589810
http://library.artstor.org.ezproxy.wesleyan.edu/library/secure/ViewImages?id=8C
    JGczI9NzldLS1WEDhzTnkrX3kucFx9cCc%3D&userId=hzBH&zoomparams=
Also: http://www.caravaggio.org/the-sacrifice-of-isaac.jsp#prettyPhoto

## ANALYZING FREDERIC CHURCH'S *THE HEART OF THE ANDES* WITH JOSEPH ADDISON'S NEOCLASSICAL AND PROTOTYPICAL THEORY OF ARTISTIC CRITICISM

*Matthew Kim*

Although the notion of the sublime in art came to prominence in the Romantic era as a particular focus of the poet William Wordsworth (1770–1850), the earliest conceptions of the sublime predate the Romantic era and may be traced to the writing of Joseph Addison (1672–1719) at the beginning of the eighteenth century. Beginning with the *Spectator* issue number 411 published Saturday, June 21, 1712, Joseph Addison began a philosophical inquiry into the particular form of human pleasure that results from the sense of sight and its playing upon the imagination. Addison introduces his topic thusly:

> Our sight is the most perfect and most delightful of all our senses. It fills the mind with the largest variety of ideas. . . . It is this sense which furnishes the imagination with its ideas; so that by the pleasures of the imagination or fancy (which I shall use promiscuously) I here mean such as arise from visible objects, either when we have them actually in our view, or when we call up their ideas in our minds by paintings, statues, descriptions, or any the like occasion.[1]

In a series of eleven essays published in the *Spectator* June 21—July 3, 1712, Addison explores the causes—as he sees them—of the human pleasure that proceeds from beholding art. His study lays out early conceptions of the sublime in art, later expanded upon by writers like Samuel Johnson, Edmund Burke, and, most notably, John Ruskin. Frederic Edwin Church was heavily influenced by the writings of Ruskin, who in turn was influenced by Burke, Johnson, and Addison. Addison therefore plays a key role in founding the prestigious line of art criticism culminating in John Ruskin and his influence on Frederic Edwin Church (1826–1900). My goal in this paper is to study Joseph Addison's seminal ideas on greatness in art, and how those ideas appear directly or indirectly almost 150 years later in Church's 1859 masterpiece, *The Heart of the Andes* (1859, oil on canvas). Specifically I will seek to answer Addison's dilemma regarding the interdependence between the artist and nature itself—how the artist may be reconciled to the raw power of nature far greater than anything a human could hope to create. I will study this question in relation to Church's work, using Addison as a critical guide.

Addison begins his study of the experience of art with an enumeration of the various powers that great art has over the human emotions. He holds up art as an entity with powers over the human mind equal to philosophical law, "a beautiful prospect delights the soul, as much as a demonstration; and a description in Homer has charmed more readers than a chapter in Aristotle."[2] Yet Addison also acknowledges the inexplicable method by which art operates over the human soul. On the visceral nature of experiencing art he writes, "We are struck, we know not how, with the symmetry of any thing we see, and immediately assent to the beauty of an object, without enquiring into the particular causes and occasions of it."[3] On an emotional level, the grandeur of Church's *The Heart of the Andes* certainly strikes one immediately and inexplicably. Standing at almost six feet by ten feet, the work's sheer massiveness awes the viewer into a kind of physical and mental submission. But apart from the measurable dimensions of the canvas, the breathtaking depiction of nature itself causes the viewer to "immediately assent to the Beauty of the Object."[4] With his description of immediate and visceral awe, Addison arrives directly at the profound conclusion that "beauty" operates by hidden and unknowable machinery to affect us, "we know not how." Viewing *The Heart of the Andes* does not necessitate prior art historical knowledge or critical theories. Each viewer will experience the artwork in a similar manner to any other human. The difference between this viewer and one who has, for example, read the complete works of John Ruskin, is that the Ruskin reader will have an heightened intellectual context in which to place the work. Prior or additional knowledge may enhance the pleasure of the viewer, but the work's success does not depend on the viewer having prior knowledge. The work must be able to stand unaided by the viewer's previous studies.

Upon concluding his introduction to the topic and preliminary observations, Addison moves directly into his prototypical articulation of the sublime. He writes on the pleasure of beholding objects that inspire terror or disgust without losing their power to please:

> There may, indeed, be something so terrible or offensive, that the horror or loathsomeness of an object may over-bear the pleasure which results from its greatness, novelty, or beauty; but still there will be such a mixture of delight in the very disgust it gives us, as any of these three qualifications are most conspicuous and prevailing. . . . Such are the prospects of huge heaps of mountains, high rocks and precipices where we are not struck with the novelty or beauty of the sight, but with that rude kind of magnificence which appears in many of these stupendous works of nature.[5]

The "horror or loathsomeness" of Church's work is in its power to dwarf one's sense of self-worth. The immensity of the central mountains and the forbidding height of the snowcapped peak in the left background render the human subjects in the middle foreground almost invisible. The power of Church's mountains proceeds not from "novelty" but from the "rude kind of magnificence" with which the mountains dominate the viewer's psyche. Further, Church's realistic portrayal of the mountains—informed by his firsthand experience with the mountains of South America—heightens the scene's magnificence by convincing the audience that such a spectacular view might truly exist in nature. The scene is not melodramatically or emotionally overwrought in such a way as to detract from the work's realism. Somehow Church has contrived to make an impossibly grand scene appear natural and possible—if he had strayed into the melodramatic the work would have lost some of its emotional power to awe. If we see the snowcapped peak in the background of the painting and determine that it looks overly enlarged, impossibly high, or otherwise unrealistic, then we cease to feel the fear that a depiction of real mountains can bring.

In his writings on pleasurable fear, specifically that which results from observing distant mountain peaks, Addison seems to speak from some personal, direct experience:

> When we look on such hideous objects, we are not a little pleased
> to think we are in no danger of them. We consider them at the same
> time, as dreadful and harmless; so that the more frightful appear-
> ance they make, the greater is the pleasure we receive from the
> sense of our own safety. . . . It is for the same reason that we are de-
> lighted with the reflecting upon dangers that are past, or in looking
> on a precipice at a distance, which would fill us with a different kind
> of horror, if we saw it hanging over our heads.[6]

Addison finds that a steep and icy "precipice" will give an observer plea-sure mainly by affirming her own safety in standing at a distance on stable ground. One wonders whether Addison ever climbed a mountain, and if he experienced the "different kind of horror" he describes that imminent danger can bring. In Church's painting, however, the mountains remain safely and comfortingly at a distance. But the snowcapped peak in the top left of the background still broods forbiddingly over the entire scene. The pure white of the summit snow, and the gentle blue backdrop of the skies, both draw the eye away from the contrastingly dark greens and browns of the rest of the scenery. Thus in contrasting light and dark, Church uses the snow covered mountain as a visual relief from the earthy color palette that dominates the rest of the landscape—especially the dark brown mountains that take up most of the center of the painting. Yet in seeking visual relief from the darker tones, we are forced to focus our attention on the "frightful appearance" of the snowy peak that would certainly "fill us with a different kind of horror, if we saw it hanging over our heads." We receive visual relief but we simultaneously must feel the pleasurable chill from fear of the distant mountain. But in Addison's estimation there is yet one more reason that we feel pleasure upon observing the awful and massive mountains of Church's painting:

> Our imagination loves to be filled with an object, or to grasp at any thing that is too big for its capacity. We are flung into a pleasing astonishment at such unbounded views, and feel a delightful stillness and amazement in the soul at the apprehension[s] of them. Such wide and undetermined prospects are as pleasing to the fancy, as the speculations of eternity or infinitude are to the understanding.[7]

Certainly in Church's painting the mountains dominate the view and the imagination. Indeed, Church depicts the mountains as extending out to the left and right much farther past the edges of the painting, which gives the viewer a sense of "wide and undetermined prospects," continuing to create an unknown vastness. It is this sense of incomprehensible size that Addison describes—the emotions that accompany one who observes something infinite in comparison to oneself. Fascinatingly, Addison describes the apprehension of such objects that are "too big for its [the Imagination's] capacity" as a feeling of "delightful stillness and amazement" rather than one of consternation and fear. Further, Addison describes the feeling as emanating from the "soul" rather than from the body. We infer, then, that the fear Addison described earlier resulted from fear of bodily harm rather than from some fear for the spirit. The feeling of calm in the face of "eternity" that Addison experiences has some echoes in Mark Twain (1835–1910) over 150 years later, though we cannot know whether Twain had Addison in mind. Still, one finds an interesting similarity in the two great writers' emotional responses to objects "too big for the imagination's capacity." Twain writes in *A Tramp Abroad*:

> One had the sense of being under the brooding contemplation of a spirit, not an inert mass of rocks and ice—a spirit which had looked down, through the slow drift of the ages, upon a million vanished

races of men, and judged them; and would judge a million more—and still be there, watching, unchanged and unchangeable, after all life should be gone and the earth have become a vacant desolation.[8]

The "unchanged and unchangeable" durability of the mountains seems to be some comfort to Twain, as they are objects to which one can anchor the psyche. Addison seems to be writing of a similar sentiment when he describes pleasure resulting from "the speculations of eternity or infinitude" that often accompany one's observation of incomprehensibly massive objects.

In his next essay Addison expands his idea of the sublime and adds to it a religious feeling of awe at God's power.

> Our admiration, which is a very pleasing motion of the mind, immediately rises at the consideration of any object that takes up a great deal of room in the fancy, and by consequence, will improve into the highest pitch of astonishment and devotion when we contemplate his nature, that is neither circumscribed by time nor place, nor to be comprehended by the largest capacity of a created being.[9]

The sublime, for Addison, directly results in reverence for God. When one beholds the beauty and power of creation at work in nature, one cannot but feel the hand of one who "is neither circumscribed by Time nor Place." In Addison's understanding of art, God is the source of one's feelings of pure astonishment when one sees an incomprehensibly massive mountain peak. Twain has a similar religious reverence—though he does not explicitly name God—in his sensation of being judged by an "unchanged and unchangeable" being. In Church's painting, the cross is the one object that stands out—without any need for massiveness or other physical prominence. Church depicts a cross inconsequentially small in comparison with the backdrop of the mountains. Yet due to its bright, almost glowing white color, and its placement directly in front of more darkly hued foliage, the cross stands out as one of the painting's most prominent objects. The saturated red and blue colors of the clothing that the tiny human subjects wear further draw the eye to the cross. One may posit many interpretations of the small cross standing before the mountains. From the perspective of Addison, one might argue that because of the infinite and incomprehensible being of God, any representation—from a tiny cross to a huge mountain—would have no ability to communicate God's amazing nature. Thus we find the argument for a conceptual substitution in Church's work. Perhaps Church means to have the mountains themselves testify to God's awesome power. The cross is merely a human representation of religious sentiment, and so—because it proceeds from devout human hands—it has no pretensions of approximating the figure and power of God. Rather, Church lets God show himself through his own creations—the awe-inspiring mountains.

Addison develops his argument to discuss human inability to produce anything even approximating the power and beauty of nature itself. Addison writes:

> If we consider the works of nature and art, as they are qualified to
> entertain the imagination, we shall find the last very defective, in
> comparison of the former; for though they may sometimes appear as
> beautiful or strange, they can have nothing in them of that vastness
> and immensity, which afford so great an entertainment to the mind
> of the beholder. The one may be as polite and delicate as the other,
> but can never shew herself so august and magnificent in the design.[10]

Seeing a painting of the Matterhorn can never compare to the experience of seeing the Matterhorn itself. Regardless of the "polite and delicate" heights that the artist achieves, a painting will never show the Matterhorn "herself so august and magnificent in design" as would be found by direct observation. Addison above argues that by the very feebleness of human artistic media, nothing produced with them can ever hope to compare to the "vastness and immensity" of Nature's works. But Addison then backtracks to make the unexpected claim that:

> But though there are several of these wild scenes, that are more
> delightful than any artificial shows; yet we find the works of nature
> still more pleasant, the more they resemble those of art. . . . And if

the products of nature rise in value, according as they more or less resemble those of art, we may be sure that artificial works receive a greater advantage from their resemblance of such as are natural; because here the similitude is not only pleasant, but the pattern more perfect."

While Addison admits that "there is something more bold and masterly in the rough careless strokes of nature, than in the nice touches and embellishments of art," he also believes that nature somehow gains by appearing similar to preexisting artwork. That is, Addison finds natural scenes in the real world to be more beautiful the more they appear to have been laid out and planned by a masterful artist as they might have been in a painting:

> Hence it is that we take delight in a prospect which is well laid out, and diversified with fields and meadows, woods and rivers; in those accidental landscapes of trees, clouds and cities, that are sometimes found in the veins of marble; in the curious fret-work of rocks and grottos; and, in a word, in any thing that hath such a variety or regularity as may seem the effect of design, in what we call the works of chance.[12]

The human eye, according to Addison, is well pleased by the "effect of design" that does not simply scatter beautiful objects at random but that places them purposefully and with some sense of reason. But the "effect of design" cannot come on so strongly that it destroys the "bold and masterly in the rough careless strokes of nature," for then the powerful quality that nature has over artificial works is lost. Essentially, Addison argues that the natural scene must have a logical beauty that structures it, but that logic cannot become the only guiding principle of the structure—some natural disorder is necessary for maximum pleasure in viewing the work. Thus when first viewing Church's painting we find a sense of order and unification that belies closer inspection of the various chaotic elements such as jungle underbrush and tangled roots in the foreground.

When *The Heart of the Andes* is viewed as a whole, the "effect of design" appears strongly, from the perfectly placed snowcapped mountain to its tonal contrast with the massive brown of the adjacent Andes, to the trees that highlight and frame—but do not obstruct—the mountain view. Yet when one looks closer, one finds Church has masterfully exhibited the "rough and careless strokes of nature" so as to have that effect equally prominent in the piece. The exposed roots of the tree on the right lean precariously over the water, and one expects the entire section of earth and tree will topple in at any moment. The detail of the mountains, while exquisitely wrought, has only the guiding sense of a natural tectonic forma- tion—Church's hand as an artist in ordering the mountains is completely invisible.

Finally, Addison gives a description of the power an artist possesses over nature. As the artist can pick and choose various objects from various scenes, and can combine these objects in the most pleasing possible way, therefore the artist has the capability of outdoing the random scattering one finds in nature. Addison writes:

> The reader [viewer] finds a scene drawn in stronger colours, and painted more to the life in his imagination . . . than by an actual sur- vey of the scene which they describe. In this case the poet [painter] seems to get the better of nature; he takes, indeed, the landscape after her, but gives it more vigorous touches, heightens its beauty, and so enlivens the whole piece, that the images which flow from the objects themselves appear weak and faint, in comparison of those that come from the expressions.[13]

One would not find the exact scene depicted by Church anywhere in South America or in the world. Rather, one realizes that Church culled from the various perfections of nature, and combined each he found with purpose in a single work. Indeed, Church "seems to get the better of na- ture" in that the picture he creates is possibly more breathtaking than any one would come across in real life. Church depicts a perfect balance of colors, from the rich reddish browns of the Andes starkly contrasted with the pure white snow-covered peak, to the perfect blue sky, to the greens and golds of the South American jungle. In nature one might not ever find two mountains so perfectly in harmony through color, proportion, and positioning. Further, the framing trees and their green hues match perfectly with both mountains' colorings. To top everything, the clouds in Church's depiction are cooperative beyond measure, obligingly exposing the blue sky where it is needed behind the white of the snowy mountain, while obscuring the sky with a fine grey where blue would clash with the Andes' brown. As if to underscore this point, Addison concludes his study of the pleasures of sight and the imagination with the reflection:

> It is the part of a poet [painter] to humour the imagination in its own notions, by mending and perfecting nature where he describes a reality, and by adding greater beauties than are put together in nature, where he describes a fiction.[4]

He leaves open the question of whether the artist or nature itself has the upper hand in producing better works for the appreciation of humanity. While nature has the raw power to awe and astonish with its enormity and grandeur, the artist can correct any mistakes or blemishes that occur by chance in nature's production. Ultimately one finds that the two are mutually dependent. Church could not have been inspired to paint *The Heart of the Andes* without actually witnessing the Andes' power and majesty. The Andes, meanwhile, have rarely before or since had their best qualities represented to such great advantage for human appreciation. In Church's masterwork, then, we find a harmonious interdependence between artist and subject that works, as Addison says, to the benefit of both.

## Notes

1. Joseph Addison, *The Spectator, with sketches of the Lives of the Authors and Explanatory Notes, in Eight Volumes* (London: William Allason, J. Maynard and W. Blair, 1819) Vol. 2., No. 411, 65.

2. Ibid., 67.

3. Ibid.

4. Ibid.

5. *Spectator, No. 412*, 69.

6. *Spectator No. 418*, 103.

7. *Spectator No. 412*, 69.

8. Mark Twain, *The Complete Works of Mark Twain, A Tramp Abroad,* (Harper, 1907), vol. 2; 41.

9. *Spectator No. 413,* 75.

10. *Spectator No. 414,* 79.

11. *Spectator No. 414,* 80.

12. *Spectator No. 414,* 80.

13. *Spectator No. 416,* 93.

14. *Spectator No. 418,* 104.

## Images

Frederic Edwin Church (1826–1900)
*The Heart of The Andes,* 1859
oil on canvas, 66 1/8 x 119 1/4in. (168 x 302.9cm)
Metropolitan Museum Of Art
http://www.metmuseum.org/toah/works-of-art/09.95

# WORDSWORTH'S ALPS

*Elizabeth Deatrick*

Of all the Romantic poets, William Wordsworth (1770–1850) was perhaps the best equipped to write about mountains. His love of mountain climbing and keen sense of sublime imagery can be clearly observed in his famed autobiographical poem, *The Prelude*. Wordsworth describes in "Book Sixth, Cambridge and the Alps" from both versions of *The Prelude* (the 13-part 1805 version and the 14-part *The Prelude* of 1850) a trip through the Alps that he took in the fall of 1790. This was no easy hike: over the course of fourteen weeks, Wordsworth covered thousands of miles "at a rate of more than twenty, sometimes more than thirty, miles a day."[1] Nonetheless, he ound ample time to pause and observe the surrounding countryside—and to learn from its beauty. *The Prelude*'s Alps are a fascinating place, fraught with contradictions; they are simultaneously inaccessible and inviting, eternally unchanging and ever different in appearance. The slopes provide their visitors with a deep, rewarding sense of the sublime—yet travelers are constantly disappointed by what they find there. Through these contradictions, Wordsworth demonstrates a way to properly read the alpine landscape as one scales it, accomplishing a personal, internal journey as one physically travels through the mountains.

Wordsworth introduces the Alps as a place of internal struggle even before the intrepid party begins to ascend them. Upon first leaving civilization, "ere twice the sun had set/[Wordsworth and his traveling companion] beheld the Convent of Chartreuse."[2] Wordsworth presents the monastery, and its surrounding landscape (which, interestingly enough, is spoken of as an extension of the House of God—it is "the house redeemed,")[3] as problematic for travelers who would enter seeking spiritual fulfillment. The human instinct is to approach the entrance to the mountains rather militaristically, to "go forth and prosper; and, ye purging fires, / Up to the loftiest towers of Pride ascend."[4] When humans enter the mountains, they inevitably (and involuntarily) bring along their personal failings and worries of the moment—"mighty projects of the time," which seem so important to mortal beings. However, the presence of all these things associated with the ever-fluctuating present destroys the perfect isolation of the "one temple last . . . this one spot/Of earth devoted to eternity."[5]

How, then, are travelers intended to access the sublime, if they cannot bring themselves into the last stronghold of "eternity"? Wordsworth realizes in the subsequent lines that in order to fully appreciate and absorb the beauty of the natural world, one must give up the ephemeral things that make up so much of human life—thoughts of revolutionary glory and conquering pride—and allow one's self to be humbled before the mountains: "to think, to hope, to worship, and to feel,/To struggle, to be lost within himself, In trepidation."[6] If this introspection is successful, the traveler may leave behind all the problematic elements of the human drives for glory and open his soul to the world where "life's treacherous vanities" are, for a time, vanquished.[7]

Once Wordsworth and his friend finally set out on their trek, they uncover another paradoxical mountain experience: in the Alps, time seems to stand still, yet the travelers' experience of the mountains is one in which the appearance of the landscape is constantly changing. The mountains are, first and foremost, presented as symbols of eternity, in which humans can lose themselves for weeks with little knowledge of the passage of time. Yet at the same time, the landscapes seem to fluctuate or change as time passes: "And earth did change her images and forms/Before us fast as clouds are changed in heaven."[8] As Wordsworth and his friend immerse themselves in the alpine landscape, they begin to perceive an immense variety of different vistas that shift and change as time passes, and as they pass through the landscape. Shadows fall differently, and as the party travels, they perceive different mountains and different angles.

How can these two different perceptions of time be reconciled? One might argue that the perception of time in the Alps is totally dependent on human actions: the visitors have *chosen* to bring themselves, and all their mortal cares, into the "one spot/Of earth devoted to eternity."[9] In doing so, they bring their mortal perception of changing landscapes and perspectives with them: now that they have lived, for a time, in this supposed "place of eternity," and find that time still passes, they may no longer perceive the mountains as unchanging. However, this interpretation is somewhat subverted by two separate facts. First, during their voyage, the travelers' aches and pains are glossed over as if the passage of time was scarcely worth noting: "'Tis not my present purpose to retrace/That variegated journey step by step./A march it was of military speed," is all that Wordsworth writes.[10] Though the travelers do see changes in the landscape associated with the passage of time, the physical discomforts that must inevitably accompany sustained mountain climbing (fatigue, hunger, and the like) are never mentioned—as if the cares associated with the passage of time are suspended while in this realm.

A second incident involving the passage of time in the Alps further clarifies Wordsworth's position. On their way down from the Alps, Wordsworth and his companion stay the night in Gravedon, a small alpine village. The two awake in the middle of the night, but they misinterpret the sound of the nighttime church bells. Believing that dawn is near, they decide to hike out to watch the sunrise by the lake. However, the time is closer to one in the morning, and the two suffer through "the sting of insects" and "rustling motions nigh at hand" for hours by the side of the lake, waiting either for sleep or for the sunrise.[11] To the reader, it is almost as if the night never ends, as the narration of the incident finishes before the sun finally rises. This passage is notable for its description of Wordsworth's discomfort: despite the grueling nature of his trip, he rarely describes his own physical condition—especially when doing so might detract from his overall portrait of the Alps as a sublime landscape. By including details that remind the reader that he too can suffer from the same discomfort as any other person (and is emphatically *not* a disembodied narrator),

Wordsworth seems to be suggesting here that the best way to experience the mountains is with no conscious knowledge of the passage of time. Discomfort comes only when they attempt to use human markings of time (the church bells) to make a plan that is dependent on a specific event (the sunrise)—but when the travelers do not actively take note of the individual parts of their journey, they accomplish the trek with ease, "eager as birds of prey, or as a ship/upon the stretch, when winds are blowing fair."[12]

Perhaps the most surprising thing about the Alps is how many unexpected emotions Wordsworth experiences while climbing them. From the strange grief he feels upon first seeing Mount Blanc and finding it to be "soulless" (in contrast to his "living thought/that never more could be") to the further letdown of finding that he has crossed the Alps without recognizing it, the poet's explanations of his various discontents seem somewhat out of place in what ought to be a pristine, eternal realm free of the failings of humankind.[13] The cognitive dissonance seems strange, especially in a poet who elsewhere finds such comfort in the mountains.

Why include these moments of disappointment? For most of his mountain trek, Wordsworth reports experiencing the exact kind of awe that he craves so deeply—it is easy enough for him to personify and wonder at elements of the landscape. He finds that the beauty of the mountains is well suited to a view of the world in which certain landscapes radiate sublime glory, which is easily understood and absorbed by humans who are ambitious enough to seek it out. Given his successes elsewhere, it seems unlikely that Wordsworth is simply suffering from an intermittent case of unreasonable expectations. Rather, the dissonance stems from the reality of climbing the Alps colliding with Wordsworth's Romantic sensibilities and ideals of what the mountains must represent—specifically, when he fails to experience the epiphany that, from a narrative perspective, would naturally occur upon having accomplished something great. Crossing the Alps, for example, should have brought him a moment of joyous realization, yet no such moment occurs. Wordsworth, for the most part, experiences "a continuity of self by participating in a series of epiphanic moments in which nature so influences the mind and impresses the soul with quietness and beauty that it cannot be adversely affected by the harsh, unsympathetic world of everyday mortality."[14] The lack of an epiphany breaks this continuity, and his perceived connection with the natural world is likewise shattered, however briefly. Curiously, however, in that moment, his "Imagination . . . rose from the mind's abyss."[15] The narrator feels comforted, not abandoned: the break allows him to take stock of his mountain-climbing experiences, to conclude that the thoughts that spring from having made his trip are "their own perfection and reward."[16]

All in all, the challenges that Wordsworth encounters in the Alps are presented not as insurmountable obstacles, but as lessons in how to climb mountains in a way that allows the climber to best experience the sublime. By surrendering his pride and conquering spirit, allowing himself to lose track of time, and realizing that disappointment springs from the same prideful human emotions that the mountains are helping him to eliminate, Wordsworth is able to craft not only an overall image of the mountains and the realizations he had there, but a guide for future sojourners in how to replicate his experiences.

## Notes

1. Stephen Gill, *William Wordsworth: A Life.* (Oxford: Oxford University Press, 1989), 44.

2. William Wordsworth, *The Complete Poetical Works* (London: Macmillan and Co., 1888), 164; lines 417–418.

3. Ibid., 164; 456.

4. Ibid., 164; 445–456.

5. Ibid., 164; 434–435.

6. Ibid., 165; 469–470.

7. Ibid., 164; 454.

8. Ibid., 165; 492–493.

9. Ibid., 164; 434–35.

10. Ibid., 165; 489–490.

11. Ibid., 168; 712, 719.

12. Ibid., 165; 498–499.

13. Ibid., 165; 526–527.

14. Hugo Walter, *Space and Time on the Magic Mountain: Studies in Nineteenth and Early-Twentieth-Century European Literature,* (New York: Peter Lang, 1999), 19.

15. Wordsworth, 166; lines 594–595.

16. Ibid., 166; 612.

## Images

Frederic Edwin Church (1826–1900)
*Cotopaxi*, 1862
oil on canvas, 48 x 85 in. (121.9 x 215.9 cm)
Detroit Institute Of Arts
http://www.dia.org/object-info/baeac490-f496-4a17-b917-dd0216d11492.aspx

Frederic Edwin Church (1826–1900)
*The Heart of The Andes*, 1859
oil on canvas, 66 1/8 x 119 1/4in. (168 x 302.9cm)
Metropolitan Museum Of Art
http://www.metmuseum.org/toah/works-of-art/09.95

# JOHN RUSKIN, TURNER, AND THE ROMANTIC PURSUIT OF TRUTH

*Avery Chase*

In 1843, art critic John Ruskin (1819–1900) published the first edition of his multivolume *Modern Painters*, largely a response to contemporary criticisms directed at the most recent landscape paintings of J. M. W. Turner (1875–1851). Ruskin writes, in the preface of the book, "For many a year we have heard nothing with respect to the works of Turner but accusations of their want of *truth*." But Ruskin sets out to prove that "Turner *is* like nature, and paints more of nature than any man who ever lived."[1] For Ruskin, Turner's works are preeminent examples of a distinctly modern (that is to say, nineteenth-century) pursuit: to fully engage with the natural world and thus perceive its essential truths. Expressing a typical Romantic sentiment, Ruskin considers immersion in nature as the necessary means of comprehending the fundamental principles of existence. In the fourth volume of *Modern Painters*, entitled *Of Mountain Beauty*, he identifies the particular significance of the mountains as ultimate manifestations of the divine that make visible the vast scale of creation, allowing man to comprehend his relative smallness in the grander scheme, but also to understand his necessary interconnectedness with the natural world. As Ruskin explains most comprehensively in *Mountain Beauty*, the Romantic ideal of landscape painting is to convey nature as one experiences it—only then is it possible to comprehend the deepest meanings of life.

During the nineteenth century, writes art historian Kenneth Clark, "[b]oth poet and painter found nature transformed by the philosophy of the eighteenth century into a mechanical universe working under the dictates of common sense; and both believed that there was something divine that, if it were contemplated with sufficient devotion, would reveal a moral and spiritual quality of its own."[2] As a movement that arose in reaction to the anatomizing effects of the Enlightenment of the seventeenth and eighteenth centuries, Romanticism necessarily expressed itself in relation to that period of scientific investigation of the natural world. That is, Romantic artists and philosophers did not revert to pre-Enlightenment sentiment, or a medieval conception of nature as frightening and unknowable. Rather, by revising the Enlightenment project, which seemingly worked to subdue nature by dissecting its elements and coldly scrutinizing them, Romantic artists engaged with nature in order to better understand their place within nature and to grasp some higher truth that transcended statistical and quantitative evaluations. "[W]henever we want to know what are the chief facts of any case, it is better not to go to political economists, nor to mathematicians, but to the great poets," Ruskin asserts in *Mountain Beauty*.[3]

Ruskin notes that the mountains (as the wilderness in general) have been understood "so little, until lately" that "in nearly all ages of the world, men have looked upon them with aversion or with terror."[4] Yet, in his quintessentially post-Enlightenment, Romantic view, Ruskin understands that the mountains not only serve the necessary functions of "feeding . . . the rivers" and "purifying . . . the air," but that they also carry out "higher missions": they "fill the thirst of the human heart for the beauty of God's working."[5] The most awesome manifestations of the divine plan, the mountains reveal elemental truths of existence that bind together all of nature, including man. Despite their massive scale and longevity, the mountains, too, are affected by "the great laws of change, which are the conditions of all material existence":

> The hills, which, as compared with living beings, seem 'everlasting,' are, in truth, as perishing as they: its veins of flowing fountain weary

the mountain heart, as the crimson pulse does ours; the natural force of the crag is abated in its appointed time, like the strength of the sinews in a human old age.[6]

Encouraging us to consider such comparisons, Ruskin suggests that the mountains enable us to contemplate the concepts of time and mortality in a way that exceeds the human scale and carries us toward a greater and more comprehensive truth.

While the rather extensive geological surveys in *Mountain Beauty* may at first appear antithetical to Romantic endeavors, they, in fact, reveal a distinctly Romantic approach to the study of nature. They are almost entirely based on Ruskin's firsthand *intuitive* observations. He even disregards conventional nomenclature, coining his own terms to describe various rock structures, such as "slaty crystallines."[7] Most illustrative of his essentially Romantic justification for this kind of self-directed scientific inquiry, Ruskin explains that for this section of the book, he considered only the studies of Swiss scientist Horace-Bénédict de Saussure (1740–1799), for, unlike other geological writers, it was only he who "had gone to the Alps as I desired to go myself, only to *look* at them and describe them as they were, loving them heartily—loving them, the positive Alps, more than himself, or than science, of than any theories of science; and I found his descriptions, therefore, clear and trustworthy."[8] Reflecting this sentiment, Ruskin declares that the highest form of landscape painting is that which "[gives] the far higher and deeper truth of mental vision, rather than that of the physical facts."[9] Romantic expression reflects the pursuit of a reality that is truer than what realism or the literal reproduction of external facts is capable of achieving. Ideally, Romantic landscape painting represents an image of nature that has been filtered through human imagination; it presents a scene of the natural world that bears the impression of the human experience within it. Explaining the effectiveness of one of Turner's mountain sketches, Ruskin claims that though it is an abstracted version of the scene, the image is profoundly true because "Turner has perfect imaginative conception of every recess and projection over the whole surface, and *feels* the stone as he works over it."[10]

When Turner appears to modify nature in his works, accentuating the size of mountains or eliminating certain features of the landscape, it is not for the sake of improving its aesthetic qualities. As Ruskin argues, the critics who object to what seems to be the overly abstract rendering of nature in Turner's landscapes do not appreciate the enlightening value of his works: in painting nature as it appears in his mind's eye, Turner communicates the truth of human experience in the world more success-fully than any other artist before him. Turner's landscape paintings are evidence of his intense engagement with nature, his profound comprehension of the world gleaned from impassioned observation, and his willingness to allow his reasoning to be overwhelmed by emotion and the experience of the thing, which enabled him to discern the essences, to depict scenes that transcend mere literal imitation of nature in their revelation of the highest principles of existence. For Ruskin, until Turner and Romantic expression, "[l]andscape art [had] never taught us one deep or holy lesson; it [had] not recorded that which is fleeting, nor penetrated that which was hidden, nor interpreted that which was obscure; it [had] never made us feel the wonder, nor the power, nor the glory, of the universe."[11] Romantic landscape painting, then, is the ultimate science, elucidating all of creation in its pursuit of essential truth.

## Notes

1. John Ruskin, *The Complete Works of John Ruskin: Poetry of Architecture, Seven Lamps, Modern Painters* (New York: National Library Association), preface to the second edition, xlvii.

http://www.gutenberg.org/files/29907/29907-h/29907-h.htm
https://www.mirrorservice.org/sites/gutenberg.org/2/9/9/0/29907/29907-h/29907-h.htm Web. 8 June 2016.

2. Kenneth Clark, *Landscape into Art* (New York: Harper & Row, 1976), 151.

3. John Ruskin, *Modern Painters, Of Mountain Beauty* (New York: E.P. Dutton and Co.), vol. 4; 29.

http://hdl.handle.net/2027/miua.2979979.0004.001 Web. 8 June 2016.

4. John Ruskin, *Modern Painters: Volume the Fourth Mountain Beauty*, (Boston: Estes and Lauriat, 1894), 106, 112.

5. Ibid., 104.

6. Ibid., 152.

7. Ibid., 121.

8. Ibid., 485.

9. Ibid., 42.

10. Ibid., 381.

11. Ruskin, *The Complete Works*, preface to the second edition, xxiv xlvii. http://www.gutenberg.org/files/29907/29907-h/29907-h.htm accessed 8 June 2016.

# THE POWER OF THE SUBLIME IN THE MOUNTAINS

*Page Nelson*

Nature is a network of incredible forces whose might looms over all humans, but in the modern age of urbanization, we often lose sight of the true majesty of our world. The notion of the sublime in nature is a cross-cultural phenomenon that likely manifested itself long before the earliest use of the term in the first century, but the modern definition of the sublime is a shadow of the resonance it held two centuries ago. The sublime is the immense grandeur of something superior to oneself, a concept that mostly came to be associated with nature—and more specifically, for the purposes of this essay, mountains in the eighteenth and nineteenth centuries. To experience the sublime is comparable to standing reverently in the foothills of the Alps, completely overpowered by the immensity of the landform towering above. It is an incomprehensible vastness that evokes extreme fear, passion, and pleasure.

The meaning of the term "sublime" has changed over time in keeping with societal trends, but its modern meaning as a synonym for "awesome" or "magnificent" is terribly diluted from the original value of the term. The initial use of the sublime to describe the pinnacle of expression that is possible through written language is usually attributed to Longinus, a first century Greek scholar and master rhetorician. Longinus outlines three essential components: passion, compelling idea, and elevated language.[1]

One's passion and compelling idea must come naturally from within and should be spontaneous, as sublimity is the resonance of soulful feeling. Elevated language acts as a quick and jarring yet more tangible vehicle for the passion and compelling ideas to transport the audience, unsettling all of their previously conceived notions of what is magnificent. Longinus stresses the importance of the impulsivity of elevated language, as the sublime could overpower any beautifully composed literary composition with potent, pure astonishment.

Longinus's definition only extends as far as recognizing literature and rhetoric as the source for the sublime, but Irish-born philosopher Edmund Burke (1729–1797) adapts this notion to apply more generally to the human experience and the physical world in his 1757 treatise *A Philosophical Enquiry into the Origins of Our Ideas of the Sublime and Beautiful*. For him, the sublime is something that is capable of producing the strongest, highest possible form of emotion, which is a coexistence of pleasure and pain, fear in tandem with immense solitude. In his treatise, he explores the interactions and distinctions between the sublime and beauty. Beauty is a more intimate impression. It is a force that provides us pleasure and draws us in, often triggering a desire for closeness. Beauty is an object of lust, which is sometimes fulfilled. This is where a divide forms between beauty and the sublime; you can scale a mountain but you can't ascend the sublimity of that mountain. The sublime is always superior to us.[2]

George Barrell Cheever (1807–1890), an American minister, wrote of the grandeur and sublimity of the Alps in *Wanderings of a Pilgrim in the Shadow of Mont Blanc* (1846). Cheever equates the immense weight of his experience of the sublime at Mont Blanc to a religious experience raising an awareness of the omniscience of God:

> But the view of such a scene also makes one sensible of his own insignificance and sinfulness; it makes one feel how unfit he is for the presence of a God of such inaccessible glory.[3]

Cheever is not alone in his appreciation of nature as a means of spirituality. There is a reason that monasteries have often been established high in the mountains. There is the physical element of high elevation that people believed could bring them closer to God.

The British Romantic landscape painter J.M.W. Turner (1775–1851) created a great number of works depicting the Alps. His works in water-color are particularly apt at representing the splendor of the mountains, the washed hues imitating soft, ethereal light emanating from the heavens. His other main area of focus is the seascape; the ocean scenes seem to fall into two divisions: the pristine view from afar or tumultuous views from within the action. This is not so much the case in his mountainous works, which tend to be mostly serene depictions, even in as chaotic a scenario as an avalanche. It is a deliberate decision to illustrate these two landforms, the sea and the mountain, differently. Both offer an imminent possibility of danger, but perhaps Turner saw the mountains as such a majestic place that, even in the most perilous of moments, he retained a sense of peace with the sublime. The sea, although also incredibly vast, does not lend it-self to this control over emotions.

Centuries ago, before the development of more advanced forms of transportation and equipment, many saw the mountains as towering, impenetrable barriers. Some surely experienced the sublime duality of terror and bliss, but the general public, especially in urban areas, stayed a safe distance from the ominous dangers of the Alps. With the develop-ment of better routes and climbing technology came a rise in the popu-larity of mountaineering. This was a leisure activity of the elite, but nev-ertheless, many were aware of the notion of the sublime and sought to find it in the Alps. With the establishment of tourism in the Alps came a more widespread understanding of the sublime as it applies to the moun-tains. Burke's image of the sublime as the astonishment produced by the incredible vastness of nature survived into the mid-1800s, but quickly diminished in the latter half of the century, as the newly established re-sorts dotting the summits were overcrowded with tourists. As a result, climbers in the mountains seeking to experience the sublime were robbed of that fundamental element of solitude due to the "buzzing hives of rest-less strangers," as American writer Mark Twain (1835–1910) describes tourists in his accounts of the Jungfrau in *A Tramp Abroad*.[4] As travel increasingly became more accessible, so did the public's use of the word "sublime," which lost some of its association with each utterance by an uninspired explorer.

Around the turn of the century, many European explorers turned their attention to the Himalayas. Alpine climbers were eager to escape the crowds in Europe and began looking for new, untraversed areas to explore. British imperialism was rampant in South Asia, with presence in India, Burma, Bhutan, and Sikkim, and as a result, the English had extensive exposure to the exotic cultures of South Asia. The Himalayas were pristine peaks with a promise of wonder and challenge, an experienced alpine climber's dream. British soldier Francis Younghusband (1863–1942) led the first group of Englishmen into Tibet, an experience that left him in a state of bliss. He had entered Tibet with the mindset of a conqueror and left with a newfound spirituality: "the first streaks of dawn gilding the snowy summits of Mount Everest, poised high in heaven as the spotless pinnacle of the world."[5] This surprising change in character was inspired, but also challenged when Younghusband led 5000 troops into Lhasa in 1904. Tibet was the only Himalayan nation that had escaped the British touch, and the government was ready to start planning their entry. Six hundred Tibetans were slaughtered when they encountered the British Troops en route to Lhasa, bringing Younghusband's newfound mysticism into question. Shortly after this expedition, trips into Tibet were planned solely for the purpose of exploration in preparation for an attempt at conquering Everest. Captain Cecil Rawling led one of these exhibitions and was the first European to see the northern face of Mount Everest. He described a sense of the sublime greater than any other:

> Towering up thousands of feet, a glittering pinnacle of snow . . .
> a giant amongst pygmies, and remarkable not only on account of its
> height, but for its perfect form. No other peaks lie near or threaten
> its supremacy. . . . There is nothing in the world to compare it with.[6]

It was during Rawling's expedition that Lord Curzon, Viceroy of India, called for a British expedition to Mount Everest, but the outbreak of World War I delayed their plans.

Many prominent European explorers went off to fight in the war, and upon their return showed profound, unprecedented psychological effects of war. John Noel, who had served in WWI, related his experience of the Himalayas to other soldiers, knowing that as they heard about the wonders of the Himalayas, they too might "know what the vision of Everest had become, at least for him: a sentinel in the sky, a place and destination of hope and redemption, a symbol of continuity in a world gone mad."[7] The battles fought in the Alps had perhaps tainted the pristine image that was held before the war, another reason for explorers to turn their sights toward the Himalayas. With war also came a desensitization towards the imminence of death; this may in turn have lessened apprehensions for climbers entering the daunting traverses of Everest. British Colonel George Mallory led the first two expeditions with the intent to ascend Everest in 1922 and 1924. Sadly, Mallory and his companion Sandy Irvine met their deaths during the second attempt, but in the most dignified way possible. Bently Beetham, one of the men from Mallory's party, eloquently lamented Mallory and Irvine from a camp overlooking Everest:

[M]oonlight seems to bring us face to face with greater and more lasting ideas; it lends a touch of the supernatural to our vision. That night and with that scene in front of one, it was quite easy to realize that the price of life is death, and that, so long as the payment is made promptly, it matters little to the individual when the payment is made. Somewhere up there in that vast wilderness of ice and rock, were still two forms. Yesterday, with all the vigour and will of perfect manhood, they were playing a great game—their life's desire. Today it is over, and they had gone, without ever knowing the beginnings of decay. Could any man desire a better end?[8]

This epitomizes the capacity of the sublime to completely overcome humans, and even lead them willingly to their demise.

We measure our life experiences in terms of pain or pleasure. Whether they are physical, mental, emotional, or hypothetical, these are two intense feelings that can be used together to describe nearly any emotional experience. One step into the mountains can bring us to remember that at any moment, natural forces could bring us to our end. The Earth is armed with countless powerful, deadly forces, such as avalanches and tsunamis, that cause terror, but accompanying this fear is also a dizzying combination of wonder, thrill, peace, and insignificance, the summation of which can be encompassed by the term "sublime."[9]

## Notes

1. Paul Velde, "Fear of the Sublime," *Antioch Review* 22 (Mar. 2010): 217–231.

2. Edmund Burke, *A Philosophical Enquiry into the Origins of Our Ideas of the Sublime and Beautiful, A New Edition* (Basil: J. J. Tourneisen, 1792).

3. George B. Cheever D. D., *Wanderings of a Pilgrim in the Shadow of Mont Blanc* (New York: Wiley & Putnam, 1846), 149.

4. Mark Twain, *The Complete Works of Mark Twain, A Tramp Abroad,* (Harper, 1907), vol. 2; 31.

5. Wade Davis, "Everest Imagined." *Into the silence: the Great War, Mallory, and the conquest of Everest.* (New York: Alfred A. Knopf, 2011), 64.

6. Davis, 65.

7. Davis, 87.

8. Quoted in Davis, 554; Bently Beetham, "The Return Journey," in *Edward Felix Norton, Fight for Everest 1924: Mallory, Irvine and the quest for Everest* (Sheffield: Vertebrate Publishing, 2015), chapter 8 (Kindle Locations 2372-2377).

9. See also: Ann C. Colley, *Victorians in the mountains: sinking the sublime* (Farnham, Surrey, England: Ashgate, 2010). *The Princeton Encyclopedia of Poetry and Poetics* (Princeton: Princeton University Press, 2012). *Credo Reference.* 11 Sept. 2012. Web. 10 Dec. 2013. <http://www.credoreference.com/entry/prpoetry/sublime>.

# THE INTERSECTION OF ALPINE PASSES AND LANDSCAPE PAINTING

*Gordon Pignato*

For nearly the duration of human existence, the mountains have served as a medium between the earthly and the divine. From the birth of Zeus to Moses' journey up Mount Sinai to the Navajo's encircling the sacred La Plata Mountains, the world's sublime peaks undoubtedly inspire spiritual feelings in many of those who encounter them. For centuries, this spiritual feeling has been reflected in mountain landscape painting. While nineteenth-century Romantic paintings perhaps best encapsulated the sublimity of the mountains, the effect transcends any one style of landscape painting. Since the birth of the tradition of realistic alpine images, artists have continuously painted mountain landscapes in a manner that captures their sublimity, and thus their role as a spiritual medium.

Indeed, this assertion is hardly disputed. However, what art historians have given less attention to is precisely why artists were and are able to reproduce the sublimity mountain travelers feel so effectively. For mountain landscape observers to truly understand artists' intentions, they must understand precisely what experiences the artists are attempting to reproduce or convey. In other words, it is not enough to identify when an artist effectively conveys alpine sublimity; a true understanding of the artwork requires knowing exactly why both the artist and the audience agree such a sublime tone exists. This author asserts that a sublime—and thus spiritual—tone is created specifically from artists' and audiences' experiences traveling alpine passes. Specifically, the lighting, content, and perspective of most mountain landscape paintings are directly influenced by the anticipation, awe, and spirituality travelers feel when traversing a mountain pass.

With modern technology, alpine travel has become significantly easier. However, passes continue to be the primary routes taken when venturing into the mountains, and are therefore the most common place of exposure to alpine scenery. A particularly effective way of analyzing how passes affect travelers is by comparing them to peaks. William Martin Conway observes that while peaks are things to be looked at, passes are places to look from. While not "conspicuously beautiful," passes are more of an experience than a sight. Passes also lead to immensely finer scenery than one would encounter while climbing a peak, as ascending a peak requires one to constantly face the slope in front of them, and leaves precious little time to relax and enjoy the view behind.[1] Meanwhile, passes offer views of long, immense ranges on either side, and—more importantly—usually display constantly changing scenery.

While a peak is already revealed to the climber, ahead of every pass lies a revelation.[2] As an 1852 edition of *The Home Friend* magazine observes, every pass offers an opportunity to "discover an unexpected and immense prospect."[3] Unlike a peak, where the route of descent is usually the same as the route of ascent, a pass is an exercise in discovering the unknown, and inspires questions: What waits on the other side? Where will we come out? What difficulties will we encounter along the way?[4] This is especially true when traveling a pass for the first time, and is enhanced by the distinct culture on either side of the pass. As Conway writes, "the contrast in scenery enforces the charm in either outlook."[5] Moreover, even one side of a pass, when the entire duration is encompassed, offers travelers new people and new surroundings: an exercise in unfamiliarity. This unfamiliarity trains the eye to better identify the differing complexities of both architecture and nature.[6]

When the chaos of a pass is combined with its often frightening and treacherous nature, it naturally becomes a spiritual medium to travelers.

*The Home Friend* notes that the unfamiliarity of passes makes them notoriously dangerous, and often reveals to travelers both their powerlessness in the face of nature and their most basic human instincts. When trouble arrives on a pass, "the son never waits for the father, nor the father for the son."[7] Meanwhile, the changing scenery evokes a sense of confusion, while every bend induces anticipation. Rapidly changing weather juxtaposes sublime softness with ferocious winds: "The traveler, humbled by the sense of nature, and awed by the majesty of nature, can scarcely fail to recognize the wonder-working power of the divine-hand."[8] Passes, therefore, combine sublimity with their humbling and anticipation-evoking nature to give mountain travelers the spiritual feelings so often associated with the mountains, and found in mountain landscape paintings.

Instead of just describing the techniques artists use to convey the feeling alpine passes evoke, it will be more useful (and display the diversity of the artwork in which the techniques are utilized) to closely examine a few paintings, and then identify common trends between the artists. *The Hunters in the Snow* (1565, oil on wood) by Pieter Bruegel the Elder (1525–1569) offers an excellent place to begin, as casual observers might not associate it with mountain passes. However, the painting includes many characteristics that lend credence to the theory that mountain passes inspired its sublimity. First, the perspective of the viewer is crucial. Unlike the hunters on the ground, who are looking down and shielded by trees, the viewer has an elevated view of the entire valley. When a viewer encounters the painting for the first time, the feeling they experience may be similar to arriving at the top of a hill (or out of a forest) and seeing everything below. The painting clearly evokes a sense of majesty at the scene stretched before the viewer, as often occurs when finally arriving at the top of a pass.[9] The painting also has a paradoxical sense of energy and calmness, as the bustling people combine with the jagged combination of diagonals in the distant mountains to create tension, while the snow on the branches in the foreground provides a sublime stillness to the artwork. It is likely no coincidence that Bruegel effectively conveyed the sense of awe inspired by the mountains by provoking feelings commonly experienced on passes.

In the painting *Ravine Between Rocks* (1630, oil on oakwood), Dutch artist Joos de Momper the Younger (1564–1635) uses different strategies to elicit the same feelings in viewers. Once again, the placement of the viewer is crucial, as Momper places the viewer in a small gorge, confining the view to the rocky walls and a narrow, hinting glimpse of the forest beyond. The lighting enhances the implicit tease of what awaits outside the gorge, as the dark foreground is just out of reach of the sunlight piercing the gorge from beyond the walls. However, the anticipation the viewer feels is again counteracted by stillness, as a sense of calm permeates the painting, transforming the energy of anticipation into something more spiritual, and recreating the feelings viewers (and Momper) have likely felt on passes.

Caspar David Friedrich (1774–1840), along with his Romantic contemporaries, possibly perfected the representation of the sublime, conveying an emotional response to mountains that closely approximates the emotions travelers experience traversing alpine passes. In *Riesengebirge* (*Landscape With Rising Mist*, 1819/1820, oil on canvas), Friedrich again uses perspective, lighting, and a paradoxical combination of energy and stillness to create the sublime and spiritual feelings mountain-lovers cherish. Like Bruegel, Friedrich places the viewer in a high location, with a majestic view of a small valley and large mountains in the background. However, Friedrich teases the viewer by using a hill in the foreground to partially obstruct the view, and illuminates the mountains in the distance to create a longing to encounter what lies within them. Both a still tree in the foreground and relatively symmetrical diagonals provide stability to counteract the energy of the swirling fog in the valleys. As in the other paintings, Friedrich's work effectively captures the feelings passes produce when traversed.

Of course, a glimpse into three paintings does by no means provide sufficient insight into the link between passes and mountain landscape painting. After all, landscape painting encompasses numerous styles, techniques, and eras. However, the commonalities of the paintings analyzed here (the use of lighting and perspective to create anticipation, the placement of the viewer, and the paradoxical contrast between energy and stillness, to name a few), seem to permeate a wide variety of mountain landscape artwork, and reflect the sublime and spiritual feelings mountain passes inspire among travelers. Such a link can provide valuable insight into the intentions of artists, perhaps revealing deviations from strategies to provoke certain feelings or, alternatively, an effort to especially focus on one aspect of the emotional relationship between humans and the mountains. More broadly, to know the specific experiences that either inspire an artist or evoke certain emotions in a painting's viewers is to gain a deeper understanding of the complexities of that painting. Too often, art historians and casual viewers alike seem to take the feelings mountains evoke as something that just happens, and enjoy them without thinking critically about what specifically provoked those feeling. Indeed, the answer is embedded in how mountains are most commonly traversed: through passes.

## Notes

1. Sir William Martin Conway, *The Alps* (London: A. and C. Black, 1904), 177–178.

2. Ibid., 179.

3. Society for promoting Christian knowledge, "Mountain Passes," *The Home friend; a weekly miscellany of amusement and instruction* (Oxford University Press, 1852), 380.

4. Conway, 181.

5. Ibid., 196.

6. Ibid., 197.

7. proverb quoted in: Society for promoting Christian knowledge, "Mountain Passes," *The Home friend; a weekly miscellany of amusement and instruction* (Oxford University Press, 1852). 382.

8. Ibid., 382.

9. Conway, 179.

## Images

Joos de Momper the Younger (1564–1635)
*Ravine Between Rocks,* 1630
oil on oak, 65.5 x 49.5 cm
Kunsthistorisches Museum Wien
Wesleyan University, ARTstor ID 40-04-03/ 7
http://library.artstor.org.ezproxy.wesleyan.edu/library/secure/ViewImages?id=
%2FThWdC8hIywtPygxFTx5RnguXX4sfFk%3D&userId=hzBH&zoom
params=

Pieter Bruegel the Elder (1525–1569)

*The Hunters In The Snow / Return Of The Hunters,* 1565

oil on oakwood, 117 x 162 cm

Kunsthistorisches Museum, Vienna

Wesleyan University, ARTstor ID 40-02-03/31

http://library.artstor.org.ezproxy.wesleyan.edu/library/secure/ViewImages?id=
%2FThWdC8hIywtPygxFTx5TnQkVnoveQ%3D%3D&userId=hzBH&zoom
params=


Caspar David Friedrich (1774–1840)

*Riesengebirge (Landscape with Rising Mist),* 1818–1820

oil on canvas, 54.9 cm (21.6 in). Width: 70.4 cm (27.7 in)

Neue Pinakotek, Munich

Wesleyan University, ARTstor ID 15812

http://library.artstor.org.ezproxy.wesleyan.edu/library/secure/ViewImages?id=4j
EgcjQrIFhfKi83cVEXRn8mVH4pew%3D%3D&userId=hzBH&zoomparams=

Also: http://www.pinakothek.de/caspar-david-friedrich-1774-1840-riesengebirgs
landschaft-mit-aufsteigendem-nebel-um-181920


For maps please see:

Walter Woodburn Hyde, 1871-1966. *Roman Alpine Routes: With Map Showing Chief Roman Passes.* 2; 2. Vol. Philadelphia: The American Philosophical Society, 1935.

# TERRIBLE BEAUTY: ARTISTIC REPRESENTATIONS OF THE WHITE MOUNTAINS IN THE NINETEENTH CENTURY

*Peter Helman*

As sites of both terrible danger and incredible beauty, the mountains have captivated artists for ages, inspiring and serving as subjects for painters, writers, and poets. In "The Notch of the White Mountains" from "Sketches from Memory," Nathaniel Hawthorne (1804–1864) writes, "They are majestic, and even awful, when contemplated in a proper mood. . . . Mountains are Earth's undecaying monuments."[1] By examining representations of New Hampshire's White Mountains throughout the nineteenth century, one can trace a shifting perception of the mountains and the creation of an artistic culture centered on the sublimity of the wilderness.

Nathaniel Hawthorne's short story "The Ambitious Guest," first published in *The New-England Magazine* in June 1835, was based on a tragedy that occurred in the White Mountains.[2] On August 28, 1826, Samuel Willey, Jr., his wife, their five children, and two hired helpers were killed by a landslide in an area now known as Crawford Notch.[3] During the avalanche, they fled their house to evacuate to a nearby shelter that they had constructed. Ironically, however, the avalanche divided in two just above their house, thus killing the Willeys while leaving their home completely unharmed. This event, referred to as the "Willey Disaster," received extensive news coverage and captured the public imagination, and as an example of the destructive power of nature, became the subject of works by contemporary artists.

The Willey family—unidentified by name—is reconstructed by Hawthorne as a microcosm of humanity as a whole: "The faces of the father and mother had a sober gladness; the children laughed; the eldest daughter was the image of Happiness at seventeen; and the aged grandmother . . . was the image of Happiness grown old."[4] Every stage of life is represented within the family. At the very beginning of the story, these happy people are placed in opposition to the natural world: "The daughter had just uttered some simple jest that filled them all with mirth, when the wind came through the Notch and seemed to pause before their cottage—rattling the door, with a sound of wailing and lamentation, before it passed into the valley."[5] The wind is personified as a spirit of death, its "wailing and lamentation" in stark contrast to the Willeys' "mirth," foreshadowing their eventual fate at the hands of the mountain. Soon, a traveler joins them, the titular ambitious guest, who declares,

[A]s yet, I have done nothing. Were I to vanish from the earth tomorrow, none would know . . . that a nameless youth . . . passed through the Notch by sunrise, and was seen no more. . . . But I cannot die till I have achieved my destiny. Then, let Death come! I shall have built my monument . . . it is our nature to desire a monument, be it slate or marble, or a pillar of granite, or a glorious memory in the universal heart of man.[6]

Here, the young guest articulates the main theme of the story: human mortality and the desire to be remembered.

Soon, of course, the lives of the traveler and the family are cut short by "'The Slide! The Slide!' The simplest words must intimate, but not portray, the unutterable horror of the catastrophe."[7] The narrator's phrasing portrays the landslide as an element of the natural world that is beyond human comprehension and articulation. And while the Willeys' "bodies were never found," the narrator asks, "Who has not heard their name? The story has been told far and wide, and will forever be a legend of these mountains. Poets have sung their fate."[8] Thus, the mountains themselves become the Willeys' monument. The closing lines of the story, however, announce,

> There were circumstances which led some to suppose that a stranger had been received into the cottage on this awful night, and had shared the catastrophe of all its inmates. Others denied that there were sufficient grounds for such a conjecture. Woe for the high-souled youth, with his dream of Earthly Immortality! His name and person utterly unknown; his history, his way of life, his plans, a mystery never to be solved, his death and his existence equally a doubt! Whose was the agony of that death moment?[9]

In the conclusion of "The Ambitious Guest," Hawthorne points to the duality of the mountains' power to create and destroy. While the Willeys are granted immortality in history and art, the traveler suffers the ultimate death of being forgotten, the fate he most dreaded, and becomes a symbol of human insignificance when confronted with the majesty of nature.

Thomas Cole (1801–1848), the artist generally agreed to be the originator of the style that came to be known as the Hudson River School, also chose the Crawford Notch—the location of the Willey family's demise—as the subject of his 1839 painting, *A View of the Mountain Pass Called the Notch of the White Mountains* (oil on canvas).[10] Cole made three trips to the White Mountains "to experience at first hand the rugged beauty of the American wilderness:" one in 1827, one in 1828, and one in 1839, and he kept journals and diaries documenting all of them.[11] In his diary entry for October 6, 1828, Cole writes, "The site of the Willey House, with its little patch of green in the gloomy desolation, very naturally recalled to mind the horrors of the night when the whole family perished beneath an avalanche of rocks and earth."[12]

In *A View of the Mountain Pass Called the Notch of the White Mountains,* Cole explores the relationship between man and nature. Near the bottom of the canvas, slightly right of center, are a small wooden shack and a man on a horse, both utterly dwarfed by the enormity of the landscape. The man's back is to the viewer, stripping him of a face and an identity (reminiscent of the death of the traveler in "The Ambitious Guest"). The wooden shack, placed next to a dead tree in a patch of grass littered with stumps, is perhaps a representation of the Willey house; it appears to be falling apart, another symbol of human death.

The composition of the painting is highly symmetrical, drawing the eye of the viewer to the distance in the center of the painting where the trees open up to reveal a bluish mist. Out of the mist rises a massive peak that dominates the frame, bathed in clouds, showing the sublime power and divinity of the natural world. The scene is set in autumn, and the leaves of the trees are changing. While the forest to the right looks somewhat dark and foreboding, the left side of the painting is illuminated by a diffuse light, and the warm oranges and reds of the trees seem to glow, constructing a duality between the beautiful and frightening elements of nature. As Cole writes in his 1836 "Essay on American Scenery" for *American Monthly Magazine,*

> [In] the mountains of New Hampshire there is a union of the pic-
> turesque, the sublime, and the magnificent; there the bare peaks
> of granite, broken and desolate, cradle the clouds; while the vallies
> [sic] and broad bases of the mountains rest under the shadow of
> noble and varied forests . . . in some regions of the globe nature has
> wrought on a more stupendous scale, yet she has nowhere so com-
> pletely married together grandeur and loveliness . . . the sublime
> melting into the beautiful, the savage tempered by the magnificent.[13]

While Hawthorne's portrayal of the White Mountains focuses more on the destructive properties of nature, Cole introduces the element of beauty and thus attains the sublime through a combination of loveliness and desolation.

In addition to expressing nature's effect on man, the image expresses man's effect on nature. A man-made path traverses the canvas, reflecting the concept of man's triumph over nature. The man on a horse is riding along the path from the dark, twisted, leafless tree in the bottom right corner to a house half-hidden by trees but clearly inhabited, with smoke emerging from its chimney—he is riding from death to life. Tree stumps, including several prominent ones in the foreground, cover the ground: they are cut evenly, so they seem to have been chopped down by men. Thus, Cole's scene establishes a dialectical relationship of life and death between man and nature: man exerts his will over nature, but nature also dominates man.

John Frederick Kensett (1816–1872), an American landscape painter identified with the second generation of the Hudson River School, also painted several scenes of the White Mountains.[14] Mark Sullivan in "Meaning in John F. Kensett's "October Day in the White Mountains," shares a letter Kensett wrote to his sister Sarah in 1850 on the subject of a trip to the Crawford Notch:

> We found much to interest and admire and much that struck us with awe and wonder. . . . In the recesses of these mountain fastnesses one cannot but be impressed with gigantic magnitude of God's work . . . the desolate character of that portion from the Willey house where the great slide of 1826 took place to the Notch is marked and impressive, and a sternness and a savage gloom hangs over the place that startles even the careless and superficial observer to awe.[15]

Kensett's writing on the subject reflects themes found in the work of both Nathaniel Hawthorne and Thomas Cole. Kensett's *October Day in the White Mountains,* painted in 1854 (oil on canvas), though, does not use the Willey house or the Crawford Notch as its subject. Instead, "viewers find themselves standing in the so-called Green Hills, to the northeast of the town of Conway. . . . We are looking south by southwest, across the Saco River . . . to Moat Mountain on the right and Mount Chocorua on the left."[16]

In some ways, however, despite their differing subjects, the composition of *October Day in the White Mountains* reflects that of Cole's *A View of the Mountain Pass Called the Notch of the White Mountains.* Both feature bodies of water in the foreground, both contain horsemen riding along a horizontal path across the frame, and both depict the White Mountains in autumn. Crucially, however, Kensett's work contains the beauty but lacks the darkness, the terror, and the tension between man and nature present in Cole's vision of the White Mountains. While Cole places a leafless, black tree in the lower right corner of his canvas, the tree in the lower right corner of Kensett's still has some of its leaves. It looks beautiful and hopeful, not deathly. While Cole's mountain juts forth, blocking out the sky, Kensett's peaks recede gently into the distance. The trees all glow with a soft light, and the composition of the painting opens out from the trees onto a hazy, infinite horizon. The minimal depiction of the sky in the top half seems to suggest Kensett's later development of the style now referred to as luminism, "characterized by broad, flat areas of smoothly applied paint that suggest the shimmering quality of atmospheric light, a careful and deliberate arrangement of forms in precisely ordered planes of spatial recession, and the experience that time and motion are immobilized."[17]

Edmund Burke argues, in his 1757 *A Philosophical Enquiry into the Origins of Our Ideas of the Sublime and the Beautiful,*

> The passion caused by the great and sublime in *nature* . . . is Astonishment; and astonishment is that state of the soul, in which all its motions are suspended, with some degree of horror. In this case the mind is so entirely filled with its object, that it cannot entertain any other, nor by consequence reason on that object which employs it. Hence arises the great power of the sublime . . . the inferior effects are admiration, reverence and respect.[18]

And in "American Landscape: Changing Concepts of the Sublime," Barbara Novak writes,

> The late eighteenth century sublime, interpreted largely in terms of Burke's definition, was associated with fear, gloom, and majesty . . . The sublime was primarily aesthetic, and to experience it was to have an aesthetic reaction. Though this reaction provoked intimations of infinity and thus of deity and the divine, it was an awesome and overwhelming divinity, dwarfing the observer who, though he aspired to transcendence, seems rarely to have forgotten his own insignificance. Such humility inspired awe. . . . This older romantic-Gothic sublime endured well into the nineteenth century in American landscape painting.[19]

This aspect of the sublime in the mountains is most clearly represented by Hawthorne's portrayal of the landslide that doomed the Willeys. This "romantic-Gothic" interpretation can also be found in Thomas Cole, but balanced with a more peaceful, warm beauty. Later, Kensett's panoramic landscape offers a view of an awe-inspiring infinite through the horizon, but it is wholly harmonious rather than terrible. As a contemporary art critic said of his work, "Mr. Kensett has long been accepted as a most consummate master in the treatment of subjects full of repose and sweetness. . . . The subdued tone of the autumnal atmosphere is singularly harmonious; how . . . warm the atmosphere . . . and above all, what sublime repose!"[20] Thus, artistic representations of the White Mountains give a sense of the changing aesthetic of the sublime in the nineteenth century and show a softening perception of the grandeur of nature.

## Notes

1. Nathaniel Hawthorne. "Sketches from Memory," *The Great Stone Face: And Other Tales of the White Mountains* (The Floating Press, Jul 1, 2011), 61.

2. Sarah B. Wright. *Critical Companion to Nathaniel Hawthorne: A Literary Reference to His Life and Work.* (New York: Facts On File, 2007).

3. John F. Sears. "Hawthorne's 'The Ambitious Guest' and the Significance of the Willey Disaster." *American Literature* 54.3 (1982): 354–367. JSTOR. Web. 12 Dec. 2013.

4. Nathaniel Hawthorne,,"The Ambitious Guest." *The Great Stone Face: And Other Tales of the White Mountains* (The Floating Press, Jul 1, 2011), 30.

5. Ibid., 30.

6. Ibid., 35.

7. Ibid., 45.

8. Ibid., 46.

9. Ibid., 46.

10. Ellen Sharp, "An Introduction to the Drawings of Thomas Cole," *Bulletin of the Detroit Institute of Arts* 66.1, in *A Special Issue, The Drawings of Thomas Cole* (1990): 4–5. JSTOR. Web. 12 Dec. 2013.

11. Judith A. Ruskin,"Thomas Cole and the White Mountains: The Picturesque, the Sublime, and the Magnificent. *Bulletin of the Detroit Institute of Arts* 66.1, in *A Special Issue*, The Drawings of Thomas Cole (1990): 18–25. JSTOR. Web. 12 Dec. 2013.

12. Louis Legrand Noble, *The Life and Works of Thomas Cole* (Hensonville, NY: Black Dome Press Corp., 1997).

13. Thomas Cole, "Essay on American Scenery," *American Monthly Magazine* (Jan. 1836), 1–12, reprinted in John W. McCoubrey, ed., *American Art, 1700–1960: Sources and Documents,* (Englewood Cliffs, N.J.: Prentice-Hall, 1965).

14. John K. Howat, "The Hudson River School," *The Metropolitan Museum of Art Bulletin,* New Series 30.6 (1972): 272–283. JSTOR. Web. 12 Dec. 2013.

15. Mark Sullivan, "Meaning in John F. Kensett's 'October Day in the White Mountains,'" *Cleveland Studies in the History of Art* 6 (2001): 48–61, 52.

16. Ibid.

17. Herbert R. Hartel, Jr., "Luminism, Transcendentalism, and Abstraction in the Paintings of John F. Kensett." *Notes in the History of Art* 21.4 (2002): 3–10. JSTOR. Web. 12 Dec. 2013.

18. Edmund Burke, *A Philosophical Enquiry into the Origins of Our Ideas of the Sublime and the Beautiful.* Ed. J. T. Boulton. (Notre Dame: University of Notre Dame Press, 1958), sec. 1, part 1.

19. Barbara Novak, "American Landscape: Changing Concepts of the Sublime," *American Art Journal* 4.1 (1972): 36–42. JSTOR. Web. 13 Dec. 2013.

20. Henry T. Tuckerman, *Book of the Artists,* (New York: G.P. Putnam & Son, 1867). *Google Books.* Web. 13 Dec. 2013.

## Images

Thomas Cole (1801–1848)

*A View Of The Mountain Pass Called The Notch Of The White Mountains (Crawford Notch),* 1839

oil on canvas, 102 x 155.8 cm (40 3/16 x 61 5/16 in.)

National Gallery Of Art

http://www.nga.gov/content/ngaweb/Collection/art-object-page.50727.html

John Frederick Kensett (American, 1816–1872)

*An October Day In The White Mountains,* 1854

oil on canvas, 79.80 x 123.50 cm (31 3/8 x 48 9/16 inches)

Cleveland Museum Of Art

http://www.clevelandart.org/art/1967.5

# *THANATOPSIS*: A VISION OF CHANGE IN NINETEENTH CENTURY AMERICA

*Penny Snyder*

The Hudson River School was the major landscape movement of the nineteenth century in America. The movement, formed by groups of intellectuals, businessmen and artists in New York City and the Hudson River Valley, sought to establish a uniquely American style of art, drawing from America's virgin landscape as inspiration. Thomas Cole (1801–1848) and Asher B. Durand (1796–1886) are typically thought of as the artistic leaders of the Hudson River School; the men shared a close friendship in addition to their participation in the same artistic milieu. Their bond with the poet William Cullen Bryant (1794–1878) led to a fruitful dialogue of letters, publications and art by each. When Thomas Cole died in 1848 both Bryant and Durand published highly personal responses. Durand visually articulated Bryant's poetry in his artistic reaction to Cole's death in the painting *Thanatopsis: A Landscape Scene* (1850, oil on canvas). The work suggests the power of nature as a refuge from emotional pain and from the modern worries of contemporary American society

The Hudson River School, appropriately named for the concentration of artists working in the area, was not self-proclaimed. The group was labeled, possibly by art critic Clarence Cook in 1879, to articulate the difference between artists committed to uniquely American art and a younger generation of artists being trained in Europe.[1] While the movement was indebted to European Romanticism at its inception, artists shifted from European modes of thinking and painting to the creation of American ones. Following Ralph Waldo Emerson's call to ignore the "courtly Muses of Europe"[2] the Hudson River School artists looked inward for inspiration, and forward for formal techniques. While artists such as Durand and Cole were inspired by European art, and even took trips to Europe to study the Western tradition, they focused on translating these ideas using an American visual language. Members of the movement focused on realistic depictions of the American wilderness, but often nature became a symbol with poetic or philosophical meaning. Thomas Cole frequently painted in this mode, exploring the heightened idealism of nature, but Durand and later painters moved away from this style in favor of naturalism. The American landscape was the source of inspiration for the Hudson River School, but the movement thrived on American cultural ideals. Durand wrote in 1850, "As untrammeled as he is, and free from academic or other restraints by virtue of his position, why should not the American landscape painter, in accordance with the principle of self-government, boldly originate a high and independent style, based on his native resources?"[3] The Hudson River School rejected the European academic methods of the past in order to produce art that was wholly American.

Leading intellectuals, authors, and businessmen joined the intellectual circles and clubs that made up the Hudson River School. While these clubs were often short-lasting, they facilitated the communication between members coming from diverse fields of endeavor including art to interact with each other, leading to the cross-pollination of Romantic and Transcendental ideas. Asher B. Durand, Thomas Cole, and William Cullen Bryant met through these clubs, beginning life-long friendships and close professional relationships. The Bread and Cheese Club, founded in 1820 was the preeminent club at the beginning of the Hudson River School movement. Durand and Bryant's first interactions occurred in the group, often called The Lunch Club.[4] The Bread and Cheese Club housed a group of prominent New York writers, artists, publishers and businessmen. Authors such as James Fenimore Cooper (1789–1851) rounded out the group, which met to discuss American approaches to literature, art and culture. While Cole and Bryant were already established in the New York artistic scene, Asher B. Durand was moving towards these artistic circles. His recent request to engrave John Trumbull's *Declaration of Independence* (1817–1819, oil on canvas) gave him the status necessary to be invited to the Lunch Club. Coincidentally, John Trumbull introduced Durand and Cole in 1825.

Both Cole and Asher B. Durand helped to form the National Academy of Design, a rebellion against the American Academy of Fine Arts, headed by Trumbull.[5] The National Academy of Design became a space for classes, exhibitions, and lectures by leading artists associated with the Hudson River School. While the National Academy of Design was a larger and more formal organization, more intimate clubs continued to propel the style of the Hudson River School. For example, Cole, Durand and Bryant founded the Sketch Club in 1829, an extension of the Lunch Club.[6] This club focused on the interactions between art and literature, with activities such as the translation of literary pieces into artwork by members at meetings. The unique structure of clubs allowed individuals from different intellectual backgrounds to interact, mirroring the interaction of literature and art that comprised the Hudson River School.

The intellectual circles that formed The Hudson River School were relatively hard to gain access to, but the movement was by no means closed off to the American public. The Hudson River School was actively engaged with modern American culture and the public. Many members of the Hudson River School's associated clubs were public figures, journalists, or editors. This gave the movement considerable access to the media. William Cullen Bryant's life-long career as the editor of the *New York Evening Post* afforded him the prestige and popularity, and he often published pieces related to—and that transmitted the ideals of—the Hudson River School. His role speaks to "growing importance of the press in the transmission of culture at mid-century and the reciprocal dependence of artists and publishers."[7] The Hudson River School not only responded to cultural changes through art, but was shaped and affected by the technological developments that made communication easier throughout the 1800s. For example, many of the artists published manifestos or letters, such as Asher Durand's *Letters on Landscape Painting*, with the express purpose of engaging the American public; this reflected a desire to include the American populace in their art.

William Cullen Bryant and Asher B. Durand's publication of *The American Landscape* in 1830 is an example of the urge of Hudson River School artists to make their work and ideas more accessible to the public. Bryant wrote in the prospectus to the volume, "the object of the work is to give a series of views to the more remarkable scenes of our country . . . which shall convey to him by whom these scenes have never been visited."[8] *American Landscape* was a collection of engravings of particularly beautiful scenes throughout New England by Durand and other artists accompanied by prose written or selected by Bryant. Both the engravings and Bryant's prose embodied the distinctly American view of nature that landscape was inherently tied to American culture. Many of the scenes were chosen for their historical significance, articulating a specific American history through art. For example, Robert Walter Weir's engraving of Fort Putnam at West Point features the crumbling remains of the fort, used in the Revolutionary War. The historical subject matter used in this publication is redolent with the nationalistic assumptions implicit in the Hudson River School's approach towards nature. In their depictions of the unique beauty of nature in the United States, Hudson River School artists attached American patriotism to the landscape. Bryant wrote in *American Landscape*, "Nature is not less liberal of the characteristics of beauty and sublimity in the new world, than the old."[9] The Hudson River School's resounding turn to the American landscape as inspiration implied the rejection of European scenes as well as European modes of art. Due to their engagement with American society and culture, the Hudson River artists' interpretations of the landscape can be read as expressions of American nationalism.

Even though many of their depictions of nature were steeped in nationalism, the artists were not completely in agreement with the dominant cultural modes of thought in the United States. The School was wary of urbanization and industrialization inherent to modern culture. Hudson River School renderings of nature exalted the pure, calming power of the outdoors as a response to the drastic changes and the deep unrest of the American socio-political landscape of the nineteenth century. The American public was confronted with many unsettled issues such as slavery in the territories, industrialization, immigration, urbanization and the tensions between the developed North and the agrarian South that would lead to the Civil War. While urban areas were often crowded and dirty, the plentiful outdoors were "forms of Nature yet spared from the pollutions of civilization."[10] Nature became a refuge from the stresses of urban living. As a response to this problem, parks and landscaping, especially at mental institutions, became an important part of civic planning and architecture due to their restorative capacities.[11] Furthermore, pieces of landscape art could stand in for the reassuring aspects of nature. Asher B. Durand writes, "To the rich merchant and capitalist Landscape Art especially appeals . . . with one or more faithful landscapes before him . . . many a fair vision . . . will animate the canvas . . . pleasant reminiscences and grateful emotions will spring up at every step."[12]

While Hudson River School artists, like Romantic painters in Europe, depicted the awe-inspiring and terrifying qualities of nature—or the sublime—the American artists shifted away from the sublime towards the beautiful. Whereas the sublime was associated with fear and a disquieting transcendent experience, the beautiful focused on the ameliorating forces of the environment. Artistic pieces that used themes of the sublime portrayed angular, jutting rocks, dizzying precipices, waterfalls, and overwhelming mountains, while pieces using the beautiful depicted pastoral scenes of slowly curving paths, smooth water and graceful trees.[13] The beautiful characterizes the Hudson River School's response to the political unrest and turmoil of the mid-nineteenth century.

While the solitude and beauty of nature were seen as antidotes for the suffering of the urban dweller, nature also offered emotional solace. Thomas Cole's death in 1848 marked the death of not only the leading landscape painter of the Hudson River School, but also of a dear friend to William Cullen Bryant and Asher B. Durand. The painting *Kindred Spirits* (1848, oil on canvas), Durand's first attempt to memorialize his friend in painting, was given to Bryant after his eulogy at Thomas Cole's funeral.[14] Durand uses painting to honor the three artists' close friendship and their shared reverence for nature. The trees, arching over the top of the composition, envelop the scene and draw the viewer into distant mountains. The diagonal line of the rock that Bryant and Cole stand on serves a similar purpose to move the viewer's eye towards the background. Durand's drawing in of the viewer allows the audience to commune with nature, much like the figures are doing. Nature as depicted by Durand is serene and calm; even the rocks are painted with soft lines, exemplifying the Beautiful. While the men stand on a precipice overlooking a stream, there is no implication of danger, suggesting a close and calming relationship between man and nature. Durand uses the Beautiful to immortalize Cole in nature. Bryant's and Cole's names are carved into the tree trunk in the foreground on the left. While their presence in nature and on the Earth is ephemeral, their names inscribed into the tree trunk are memorialized and endure.

Durand returned to the subject of Cole's death in 1850, painting *Landscape: Scene from "Thanatopsis."* Unlike *Kindred Spirits'* implied reference to the ephemerality of life, *Thanatopsis* (1850, oil on canvas) explicitly references death in its narrative. While *Thanatopsis* is a highly personal meditation on the death of a close friend, it also articulates the Hudson River School's use of the Beautiful to represent the calming, restorative, and religious aspects of nature. The work was exhibited at the National Academy of Design for a year, then purchased by the American Art Union.[15] This purchase suggests Durand's prominence in the Hudson River School at the time, as well as the work's resonance with the cultural sentiments of the mid-nineteenth century.[16] The painting was heavily involved with the culture of the Hudson River School in its inspiration as well as its ownership. In addition to responding to Cole's death, Durand drew from Bryant's poem "Thanatopsis" for the thematic dimension of the work. William Cullen Bryant was perhaps best known for this poem, published in 1817 when he was only seventeen. Meaning "meditation upon death," the poem explores the relationship between death and nature. Bryant rejects fear of death and celebrates life, portraying life and death as a continual process that is connected with nature. Durand quoted the following lines in the catalogue of the exhibition of *Thanatopsis* in 1850.[17]

. . . The hills
Rock-ribbed and ancient as the sun; the vales
stretching in pensive quietness between;

The venerable woods—rivers that move
In majesty, and the complaining brooks
That make the meadows green; and, poured round all,
Old Ocean's gray and melancholy waste,—
Are but the solemn decorations all
Of the great tomb of man![18]

Even though it was composed some thirty years earlier than Durand's painting, "Thanatopsis" still epitomizes many aspects of Hudson River School philosophy. For example, early in the poem Bryant establishes the power of nature to influence human emotional states, similar to later theories of the Beautiful. Nature is a calming force to those confronted with thoughts of death. He writes that "When thoughts/ of the last bitter hour come like a blight. . . . Go forth under the open sky."[19] In addition to the emotional connection between humans and nature, Bryant explores the intense connection between humans and the Earth in death. The body after death becomes part of the physical Earth; "Thine individual being shalt thou go/ To mix forever with the elements."[20] For Bryant, the body participates in the physical cycles of life and death of the Earth, but humans also become part of a larger human history of life and death. Rather than being morbid, Bryant's "innumerable caravan" of death suggests the continual process of life and death that all humans participate in. Bryant reminds of the smallness of an individual human life by evoking a greater sense of humanity. Individual human lives and deaths are small parts of the beauty of human history and of the physical Earth itself.

Durand depicts death as "pleasant dreams" in *Thanatopsis*, suggesting the calming forces of nature, and the interrelationship between humans and nature. Unlike in *Kindred Spirits* Durand explicitly references death in *Thanatopsis*. Nevertheless, although there are many reminders of death in the work, it is resoundingly optimistic. Often the images of death are accompanied by images of rebirth or renewal. The work focuses on a beautiful, idealized scene, encompassing pasture lands, a river, and mountains; it encompasses what seems like the totality of human existence in one scene. Under a darkened grove of trees, mourners gather for a funeral. The mourners are partially covered in shadow, a traditional rendering of the darkness of death, but the light that suffuses the work penetrates the trees to cover the mourners with light, speaking to hopefulness in the face of death. While the funeral is a literal reference to death, the mourners are small in scale and partially obscured by trees. By making the funeral hard to see, Durand suggests that while death is an omnipresent happening, like its small part in the painting, it is just a small part of human experience. Next to the funeral, Durand depicts a dead tree with bare, broken branches reaching pointlessly to the sky. The tree is an example of death in nature, suggesting that human death and death of plants and animals in nature are not so different. However, in the middle of the tree trunk grows thick, green foliage, an image of rebirth juxtaposed with the death of the tree trunk and the funeral. Ruins of human creation litter the ground, suggesting the transient quality of human endeavor. The ruins hide another explicit reference to death, as a human skull is buried within the ruins, near the grazing goat. The human skull is an example of a *memento mori* or reminder of death, typically used in elegiac works. The skull thus becomes a reference to Cole's death. However, Durand's depiction of the calming and religious qualities of nature counteracts the negative qualities of death. The golden, airy light of sunrise suffuses the work, a characterization of a religious dimension of nature. The light, especially juxtaposed with the human skull in the foreground, hints at reincarnation after death, or at least the peacefulness of death itself.

*Thanatopsis'* panoramic view is appropriate for Durand's exploration of the continuity of human experience. Death, daily life, rebirth all occur in one scene. Nature becomes a philosophical representation of the cycles of life and death in the work due to its grand scope. However, this runs counter to Durand's typical style of painting. Durand generally painted in the mode of naturalism, with realistic depictions of natural sites that one could actually visit and reproduce. *Thanatopsis,* by contrast, is idealized and could not exist in the real world. The Gothic castle nestled in the mountains and the Arcadian ruins hint at romanticism and may refer to Thomas Cole's painting.

By physically depicting Cole and Bryant in *Kindred Spirits*, Durand immortalizes the relationship between the artists, but in *Thanatopsis* he uses Bryant's words and Cole's style to immortalize their friendship. The embodiment of Cole in the work encompasses not only the references to death, but also the style in which Durand paints the work. Durand offers the ultimate tribute to Cole in *Thanatopsis* by subordinating his own style to Cole's.

Thomas Cole's death left an empty space in both the Hudson River School and the lives of William Cullen Bryant and Asher B. Durand. The artists' close friendship speaks to the unique structure of the Hudson River School and the intellectual culture of America in the 1800s. Their works were deeply indebted to their friendship and to their interactions with the Hudson River School. Durand replaced Cole as the unofficial leader of the movement, but the Hudson River School eventually saw its prominence wane in the latter half of the nineteenth century. However, the works of both artists, especially *Thanatopsis*, commemorate not only their friendship, but also an important moment in the creation of purely American art.

## Notes

1. Kevin J. Avery, "A Historiography of the Hudson River School," in *American Paradise: The World of the Hudson River School* (New York: Metropolitan Museum of Art: Distributed by H.N. Abrams, 1987), 3.

2. Ralph Waldo Emerson, "The American Scholar," *The American Scholar, Self-Reliance Compensation* (New York: American Book Company, 1893) 45.

3. Barbara Dayer Gallati and Fundación Juan March with the New York Historical Society, *Letters on Landscape Painting: Asher B. Durand,* (Originally published in *The Crayon 1855–1875*, Fundación Juan March, 2011), Letter II.

4. Ella M. Foshay, *Intimate Friends* (New York: New York Historical Society. 2000), 12.

5. Ibid., 13.

6. Ibid., 13.

7. Barbara Dayer Gallati, "Durand's Letters on Landscape Painting: A Modern Spirit in Context." *The American Landscapes of Asher B. Durand (1796–1886)* (Madrid: Fundacion Juan March. 2010), 205. Print.

8. Ferber, Linda S. "*The American Landscape* and the American Grand Tour." *The American Landscapes of Asher B. Durand (1796–1886)* (Madrid: Fundacion Juan March. 2010), 102. Print.

9. Ibid., 103.

10. Barbara Dayer Gallati and Fundación Juan March with the New York Histor-ical Society, *Letters on Landscape Painting: Asher B. Durand,* (Originally published in *The Crayon* 1855–1875, Fundación Juan, March, 2011), Letter I.

11. Rebecca Bedell, "Nature is a Sovereign Remedy," *The American Landscapes of Asher B. Durand (1796–1886)* (Madrid: Fundacion Juan March. 2010), 196.

12. Barbara Dayer Gallati and Fundación Juan March with the New York Histor-ical Society, *Letters on Landscape Painting: Asher B. Durand,* (Originally published in *The Crayon* 1855–1875, Fundación Juan March, 2011), Letter IV.

13. Bedell, 197.

14. Ella M. Foshay, *Intimate Friends* (New York: New York Historical Society, 2000), 12.

15. Albert Ten Eyck Gardner and Stuart P. Field, *American Paintings: A Cata-logue of the Collection of the Metropolitan Museum of Art Vol. 1. Painters Born By 1815* (New York: Metropolitan Museum of Art, 1965), 211.

16. David Schuyler, *Sanctified Landscape: Writers, Artists, and the Hudson River Valley, 1820–1909* (Ithaca: Cornell University Press, 2012), 93.

17. Gardner, 211.

18. William Cullen Bryant, "Thanatopsis," *Yale Book of American Verse*, ed. Thomas R. Lounsbury (New Haven: Yale University Press, 1912), 38–46.

19. Ibid., 8–14.

20. Ibid., 26–27.

# Images

Asher Brown Durand (1796–1886)
*Kindred Spirits,* 1849
oil on canvas, 44 x 36 inches
New York Public Library
Wesleyan University ARTstore ID CARNEGIE_4010002
http://library.artstor.org.ezproxy.wesleyan.edu/library/secure/ViewImages?id=
    8jNTaD4kJDgpRy07ej16Rg%3D%3D&userId=hzBH&zoomparams=

Asher Brown Durand (1796–1886)
*Landscape: Scene from Thanatopsis,* 1850
oil on canvas, 39 1/2 x 61 in. (100.3 x 154.9 cm)
Metropolitan Museum of Art
Wesleyan University ARTstore ID 1114
http://library.artstor.org.ezproxy.wesleyan.edu/library/secure/ViewImages?id=
    %2FDFMaiMuOztdLSowdD5%2BRnsg&userId=hzBH&zoomparams=

# THE SOUTH AMERICAN MOUNTAINS OF ALEXANDER VON HUMBOLDT AND FREDERIC EDWIN CHURCH

*Elizabeth Deatrick*

Alexander von Humboldt (1769–1859) was a truly remarkable man. As one of the foremost of the early naturalists, his scientific discoveries, combined with his eloquent writing and exciting travel experiences, served to make him one of the most influential of any of the Romantics. A squid (*Dosidicas gigas*, the Humboldt squid), a penguin (*Spheniscus humboldti*), a major ocean current (the Humboldt current, which runs along the Western coast of South America), and several major towns throughout the Americas are named after him, demonstrating Humboldt's importance not only to scientists, but also to Romantic culture at large. One of his most influential connections, however, was in the world of art: Frederic Edwin Church (1826–1900), one of America's first prominent landscape painters, was a disciple of Humboldt's. As Stephen Jay Gould writes, "When Church began to paint his great canvases, Alexander von Humboldt was probably the world's most famous and influential intellectual."[1] Driven by a desire to explore and inspired by such works as Humboldt's five volume *Kosmos* (published between 1845 and 1862), Church sought to replicate Humboldt's South American voyages, traveling in quest of sublime landscapes to paint. The resulting paintings, which include *Cayambe* (1858, oil on canvas), *The Heart of the Andes* (1859, oil on canvas), and *Cotopaxi* (1862, oil on canvas), demonstrate the degree to which Humboldt and his followers influenced Church's artistic thought.

Humboldt was no stranger to mountains before his trip to South America—as a young man he worked as the Prussian chief inspector of mines. He had extensive experience in the Fichtel Mountains, gaining knowledge of geology and its practical applications. This knowledge was brought to play on Humboldt's later South American voyages, whose scientific impact was significant. Church, following in Humboldt's footsteps, made several similar trips. While Humboldt was primarily looking for scientific curiosities, and Church sought picturesque landscapes, both of them were also seeking the sublime—and Church set out to find and paint, amongst other things, the landscapes that Humboldt found so inspiring. Humboldt's influence on Church's own experience of South America shines through in the resulting paintings. In each one, Church uses the mountains of South America (as well as other elements of the landscape, such as plants, birds, and rivers) to elaborate on and explore facets of Romantic thought—many of which Humboldt also engaged with in similar ways in his various writings.

Take, for example, Church's painting of the mountain of Cayambe, finished in 1858. The Church scholar Gerald L. Carr draws a link between Humboldt's description of the mountain of Chimborazo in Ecuador and the scene depicted in *Cayambe*, noting the parallel between the ruined Forum Romanum invoked in Humboldt's writing and the Aztec ruins in the foreground of *Cayambe*: "Humboldt had likened Chimborazo to Michelangelo's dome at St. Peter's Basilica ascending—admittedly, across town—above the ruined Forum Romana. . . . Those phrases fit Church's studio painting, *Cayambe* . . . perfectly."[2] While this visual link is reasonably accurate—the crumbling Aztec ruins in the foreground are not unlike the toppled pillars in the Forum, and the mountain looms behind like the much greater, more godly basilica—the extensive similarities between the two descriptions hardly stop there. If the Aztec ruins are equated with the work of the ancient Romans, and the mountain behind with the cathedral, another link suddenly becomes apparent: the sharp contrast between the two Romantic experiences of nature. The foreground of *Cayambe* represents the fragile, intimate, immediate concept of the beautiful: the trees and crumbled stones shaped by the work of ephemeral humanity are incredibly detailed. Individual leaves glint with different shades of red and yellow and green. A delicate, long-necked bird perches on the left-hand side, and more descend to the palm trees that sprout from the right, framing the picture in beautiful animal life.

The beauty of the foreground reinforces the immense majesty of the mountain behind, which embodies the Romantic concept of the awe-inspiring, powerful, terrifying sublime. While the painting is as detailed in the distance as elsewhere, the viewer is able to grasp (based, in part, on the height of the clouds, serving the same function as a row of rooftops) the sheer scale of Cayambe. Thanks to the flow of water towards the lake at its base, the viewer's eye is drawn towards the peak—yet at the same time, the sharp contrast between the mountain's snow and the lush, inviting jungle in the foreground gives the peak a forbidding or even openly hostile air. Even the clouds halfway up the mountain contribute to this effect: visually, they act as a wall, but the mind recognizes that they are insubstantial, and would be no barrier at all to the ambitious climber. Because of the Romantics' association of strong emotions with ultimate goals, Cayambe becomes not just a mountain, but a pilgrimage destination—a holy site that begs both adoration and a quest to attain it. Where St. Peter's is a Christian cathedral, Cayambe becomes a temple of the sublime.

The Romantic concept of the sublime in nature, however, necessarily incorporates not only the huge and ancient, but also the uncontrollable and the terrible. Frederic Church's painting of Cotopaxi, from 1862, incorporates the latter ideals to create an awful apocalyptic vision. Here, Church depicts the eruption of Cotopaxi: smoke and ash boil forth from the summit of the distant volcano, covering the sky with a haze of ash. During his trek in the Andes (and his experience with similar volcanoes), Humboldt realized, through a careful study of the geology of that region, that the creation of mountain ranges could follow the then-controversial vulcanist model: mountains, like ecosystems, could change in periods of time observable by humans, and in occasionally cataclysmic ways. As Gerard Helferich writes in his book on *Humboldt's Cosmos,* Humboldt discovered:

[T]he Andes had been created by heat, not sedimentation. More-over, the landforms were obviously recent—and still in the forming, as witnessed by the frequent earthquakes and dozens of active vol-canoes—not the product of a one-time long-ago process of creation.[3]

Although Cotopaxi was quiet when Humboldt visited it, Church's paint-ing reflects Humboldt's realization of the immediacy that the creation of mountains could take on, as well as the knowledge that geologic processes of change could be observed, by humans, in real time.[4] As the viewer's eye pans from left to right across the painting of Cotopaxi, following the direction of the volcano's billowing clouds of ash, the viewer experiences a kind of shift in geologic time. On the extreme left of the painting, the sky is clear, and tall trees appear to be flourishing. A woman leads her llama along a path at the bottom—the only sign of human life in the entire image. This corner of the piece clearly represents the modern day, but just a little to the right, the apocalypse begins with the erupting of the volcano. The pale blue of the sky is turned orange by clouds of ash and dust. The sun sets—or does it rise?—over a flooded plain, the end of which drops dramat-ically into a chasm.

But the apocalyptic vision of destruction is not the end for life in the landscape—quite the contrary. On the right side of the image, life begins to reappear, but something is different. The trees are scraggly, lacking the de-tail and size of those on the left, and the tiny white birds do not fly towards them, but down into a giant cleft in the rock. Their behavior is reminiscent of the "oil-birds," or guacharo, that Humboldt encountered fairly early in his voyage-birds which live inside a cave which "reminded Humboldt of the descent into Tartarus."[5] The experience of visiting the birds left Hum-boldt unnerved, and their presence here is telling. This is a world that has survived catastrophe, but only when the beings living in it take on behav-iors that seem almost unnatural to modern eyes.

The question that the viewer is confronted with, of course, is whether the sun is rising or setting; whether the apocalypse has already happened or is yet to come. The former invokes a massive timespan, punctuated by cataclysms—something like the theories of vulcanism that Humboldt be-lieved in and attempted to prove. The latter, however, may be more in line with the Christian concept of the apocalypse in Revelations: the forth-coming end of all things, dictated not so much by geologic forces as by the struggle between God and Satan. In either case, the painting seems to suggest a recurring cycle of cataclysm and rejuvenation of life to suit its new environment—a concept that Humboldt was fascinated by. Life may rejuvenate into strange forms, but rejuvenate it will, always better suited to its environment.

This life is on prominent display in Church's *The Heart of the Andes,* painted in 1859. In stark contrast to the desolate landscape of *Cotopaxi, The Heart of the Andes* is a deeply peaceful, verdant scene. There is human life here too, and, as in *Cotopaxi,* it is dwarfed by its surroundings. However, the two men to the left of the river are not walking away from the disaster (as the woman in *Cotopaxi* is) but instead are sitting, contemplating a white cross, as well as the landscape in front of them. While the two paintings both grapple with themes of life and death, their conclusions are clearly different: where *Cotopaxi* depicts destruction and the slow recovery from it, *The Heart of the Andes* shows a scene that, while once chaotic with fire and death, has finished its recovery, and come to an ecological stasis.

The most obvious symbol of death is the white cross in the clearing on the left of the painting. It could be a memorial or a gravestone—or merely a reminder that, once, a man died so that others might have eternal life. Just to the left of the two figures (and in front of them) a dead tree with a burned trunk adds a striking bright point. Its charred wood suggests an ancient fire, but a flowering vine twines up its trunk, signaling the new life that builds on the remains of the old. Despite the echoes of some ancient tragedy, there is no sense of doom or terror in this painting. This landscape is much closer to the classical, pastoral ideal of Arcadia than are the other two paintings: though the Andes rise up from the background, they offer no serious boundary or threat to the tiny humans, who may sit and contem-plate facts of life—and death—in peace.

"Throughout his life," writes Gerard Helferich, "Humboldt champi-oned a particular way of viewing the natural world—one that sought to cut through the apparent dissimilarities among phenomena in order to lay bare the underlying unity of all nature."[6] Church, too, included certain near-universal similarities in his paintings: certain recurring elements serve as continuity between the South American paintings. For example, all three of these paintings have rivers in the foreground, and two of those (*Cayambe* and *The Heart of the Andes*) have great cataracts plunging off of cliffs. This is a particularly apt example because, in all cases, these rivers serve to link one visual element with another—the foreground with the background—providing a sense of continuity between the viewer and the distant mountain landscape. That said, the rivers are unique in each work, and the nature of each river serves to clarify the relationship that Church wishes viewers to have with the mountains. Although Humboldt himself was more interested in the geology of mountains than in rivers, Church's inclusion of bodies of water in the vast majority of his South American mountain paintings speaks to his belief that to have such a connecting element was vital, from an artistic standpoint. Each river represents a different human way of interacting with the sublime, and all of these avenues are presented as valid in their own ways.

In *Cayambe,* for example, the river flows away from the viewer, into the valley between the viewer and the mountain. This has the effect of drawing the eye upwards, towards the mountain—further emphasizing the distant mountain as a destination or a place of pilgrimage. The water acts almost like a road which the pilgrim must follow: even though the river flows down into a valley, other streams must surely connect the distant mountain to whatever river the closer stream joins up with. The river in *Cotopaxi,* by contrast, serves more as a barrier than a road. The violence of its waterfall echoes the violence of the volcano, its erosive force serving as a counterpoint to the violent creation of the mountain behind it. Here, although the eye is, once again, drawn back towards the mountain, the waterfall creates a physical rupture in space that separates the viewer from the events in the background, reinforcing the suggestion that these events are distant in both space and time. This landscape, it seems to say, will have no mercy upon the casual human traveler. The waterfall in *The Heart of the Andes,* although similarly misty in its violence, is much smaller in relation to the surrounding mountains, and the placid lake at its base only contributes to the inviting scene in the foreground—a staging area for the valley beyond, rather than an obstacle to it. Water pours out of the mountains and down into this refuge, suggesting a transport of something vital of the mountains (a sense of awe at the world, or perhaps a measure of peace and solitude) down to this area of contemplation.

Though Humboldt's primary goal in writing about South America was that of scientific exploration and explanation, his texts were never intended to be only for the most elite of scientists. Rather, they were written in the Romantic tradition, and Humboldt did not shy away from recording his own emotions upon making particularly exciting (or, on occasion, disappointing) discoveries. His writing conveys facts, of course, but also includes a sense of wonder and excitement at the exotic wonders around him. To readers who might never have left their native lands, his vivid descriptions of climbing previously unscaled mountains and discovering exotic birds must have seemed thrilling: his own emotions bottled up, then unsealed for his audience to be recollected—by them—in the tranquility of their homes. In exploring the same regions of the world and painting them for audiences elsewhere, Frederic Church was able to give much the same experience to his viewers: his paintings convey all the wonder of distant locations and the interconnectedness of all themes and lives, as they layer symbolism of life, death, and the human place in nature.

## Notes

1. Stephen Jay Gould, "Church, Humboldt, and Darwin: The Tension and Harmony of Art and Science" in *Frederic Edwin Church*, by Franklin Kelly, with Stephen Jay Gould and James Anthony Ryan (Washington: Board of Trustees, National Gallery of Art, Smithsonian Institution Press, 1989), 96.

2. Gerald L. Carr, Frederic Edwin Church, and Berry-Hill Galleries, *In Search of the Promised Land: Paintings by Frederic Edwin Church* (New York: Berry-Hill Galleries, 2000), 67.

3. Gerard Helferich, *Humboldt's Cosmos: Alexander von Humboldt and the Latin American Journey That Changed the Way We See the World* (New York: Gotham Books, 2004), 299.

4. Helferich, 235.

5. Douglas Botting, *Humboldt and the Cosmos* (London,: Joseph, 1973), 84.

6. Helferich, *xviii*.

# Images

Frederic Edwin Church (1826–1900)
*Cayambe,* 1858
oil on canvas, 12 x 18 in. (30.48 x 45.72 cm)
Museum of Fin Arts Boston
http://www.mfa.org/collections/object/cayambe-33108

Frederic Edwin Church (1826–1900)
*The Heart Of The Andes,* 1859
oil on canvas, 66 1/8 x 119 ¼ in. (168 x 302.9 cm)
Metropolitan Museum Of Art
http://www.metmuseum.org/toah/works-of-art/09.95

Frederic Edwin Church (1826–1900)
*Cotopaxi,* 1862
oil on canvas, 48 x 85 in. (121.9 x 215.9 cm)
Detroit Institute Of Arts
http://www.dia.org/object-info/baeac490-f496-4a17-b917-dd0216d11492.aspx

# FROM POSTCARDS TO WATERCOLORS: EMIL NOLDE (1867–1956) AND THE MEDIUM OF THE MOUNTAINS

*William Wiebe*

This paper offers a chronological exploration of Emil Nolde's artistic development through his depiction of mountain landscapes, identifying a thematic consistency in his work despite the considerable evolution of his methods of depiction. After providing a brief history of Nolde's personal experiences in the mountains, the paper compares two representative mountain landscapes from the pre-expressionist stage of his career—*Jungfrau, Mönch und Eiger* (*The Virgin, Monk and Eiger*), 1894-96 and *Bergkulisse* (*Mountain Scenery*), 1897—with a work done significantly later—*Schweizer Berge (junge Frau im Vordergrund)* (*Swiss Mountains (Young Woman in Foreground)*), 1948—arguing that, in both periods, his art sought to open "the door to the forces operating beyond external appearance," even as the means by which he sought to achieve that end changed dramatically.[1]

In his late teens, Nolde left his ancestral home in northern Germany in search of employment and the opportunity to pursue his artistic passions. Having had some experience as a woodcarver, he became the apprentice of a furniture-manufacturing firm, a four-year program he followed to its completion in early 1888.[2] Dulled by his work as a journeyman, he quit his job the following winter and enrolled full-time at an arts school; after a mere two semesters, however, he had depleted his meager savings and found himself thrust back into his previous employ as a furniture designer and manufacturer.[3] This work sustained him until 1892, when he began a career teaching and drafting designs at the Museum for Industrial and Applied Arts in St. Gallen.[4] It was in this world of the Swiss Alps that Nolde, variously described as "the son of the flatlands" and "a man of the plains," found calling as "a highlands tourist," translating his inborn affection for his native countryside into a deep appreciation for his new surrounds.[5]

Nolde quickly made a habit of exploring the hitherto unfamiliar landscape: as the duration of his stay in St. Gallen advanced, so did his willingness to venture into the mountains beyond. Complementing his usual day hikes with strenuous alpine tours (including ascents of the Jungfrau and the Matterhorn), he thrust himself further into danger—and, in his opinion, into closer communion with the natural world.[6] He described to friends how, in the Alps, one found "nature in all its primitiveness . . . unaffected and mighty," the "snowcapped mountains proudly [protruding] into the sky."[7] Indeed, his affection for the mountains grew simultaneously from his Romantic predisposition and his passion for the outdoors, twin impulses that would ultimately inspire him to render the landscape pictorially, to know it as an artist.[8]

With these impulses behind him, he began work on his mountain postcards, a group of oil paintings presenting literal depictions of the characters named by different mountains in the Swiss Alps (for instance, the *Jungfrau*—"Virgin"—became a slight young maiden). By 1897 he had completed a series of thirty motifs, two of which were published by the art magazine *Jugend* the following year (when he had submitted *Bergkulisse* to the magazine as a cover design the previous year, it had been rejected).[9] At the behest of numerous collectors, Nolde borrowed the money necessary to print a large edition of the works, selling one hundred thousand cards within ten days at a significant profit.[10] This turn of fortune freed Nolde from the financial constraints that had hampered his earlier attempts at an artistic career, allowing him to quit his job in St. Gallen and take on painting full-time.[11] Indeed, many mark 1898 as the year Nolde truly began his life as a painter, when, having finally achieved the wherewithal to work professionally as an artist, he left St. Gallen for Munich.[12] In Munich he realized his desire to receive formal artistic training, studying landscape painting and familiarizing himself with van Gogh's use of "colour as an unrestrained force of spiritual and emotional expression."[13]

Thus, by the time he returned to St. Gallen, in 1924, he was well-schooled in the aesthetic and emotional power of color, now the "chief medium of his art."[14] Following his short-lived membership in the Dresden-based *Die Brücke* (which he quit due to what he perceived to be the group's creative redundancy after a mere eighteen months), he had continued to move through Germany's avant-garde circles, gaining membership in the Berlin Secession in 1908 and exhibiting with *Der Blaue Reiter* in 1912.[15] However much he relied on the artistic and commercial connections he developed during this period to support his work, he produced his work in solitude, completing the bulk of his paintings at the remote home in northern Germany where he lived for much of the year.[16]

Traveling, then, afforded a rare occasion to incorporate new geographies into his work, and the trips he took to Switzerland in the late 1920s and early 1930s were no exception. On his first return, he found his "enthusiasm for the Swiss Alpine world unbroken," remarking that he stood "almost blinded before the mountain's enormous magnificence."[17] That Nolde—chiefly, though by no means exclusively, an oil painter—recorded these journeys only through watercolors reflects the special sense he had for his time there: Fluck contends that "he did not consider oil painting a suitable medium to capture the way in which he saw and felt the beauty of the Swiss mountain landscape."[18] Taken together, the mountain watercolors demonstrate great technical proficiency and emotive depth.[19] Even as they incorporated the force of color with new freedom, these images referenced the same primitive strength of the mountains that he had sought to depict in his postcards.[20]

In *Jungfrau, Mönch und Eiger*, Nolde creates a literal personification of the eponymous mountains, inserting the visages of a virgin, monk, and ogre in place of the mountains' true faces. This figurative technique repeats throughout his mountain postcards, each of which attempts a translation of a mountain (or range of mountains, as the case may be) into a caricature of its namesake. The work is self-consciously lowbrow, marrying the grotesque figures of folklore with the splendor of the mountain world in a riff on the vernacular traditions of the Swiss Alps and comedic travel postcards popular at the time.[21] And yet, while the exercise may seem relatively straightforward, the humorous subject matter succeeds both because it builds on the solid artistic foundation Nolde provides and because it is informed by a deeper, more persistent vision of "an animated nature that slumbered in deep seclusion"—one that finds new (and less literal) meaning in his later Expressionist work.[22] By carefully blending the borders of the two worlds—that of the characters and that of the landscape—he permits the viewer to read them as one, even as his stylistic choices and use of color reinforce their separation. Nolde renders the characters in *Jungfrau, Mönch und Eiger* quite naturalistically, carefully attending to the details of their expressions while subtly drawing them out of the mountain scenery that serves as their vestments. Nolde also uses the natural position of the mountains to frame the central tension of the piece. Pushed against the dark, cool blue of the sky, the three brightly lit figures strike a stark contrast, that—together with the pyramidal compositions atop which each of them rests—immediately asserts their pictorial significance to the viewer. The rosy-cheeked monk, flanked by the two women, glances toward the coquettish virgin in a moment of temptation as the homely ogre flashes a cruel grin, the proverbial devil on his shoulder, urging him to abandon his vows. As one's eyes track down from the peaks, though, the fleshy tones of the painting's protagonists and the realistic treatment of their features melt away into a more impressionistic rendering of the natural world, where dashes of browns, whites, blue, yellows, and greens layer over one another in a frenetic burst of mark-making. This treatment of energy and color imbues the composition with an emotional depth in a manner reminiscent of his later Expressionist oil paintings. However, the density of the brushstrokes and the almost overwhelming variety of hues in this work—as well as the substance and weight of the oil paint—clearly lack the quiet poetry of his later mountain watercolors. Though the landscape prefigures Nolde's later efforts to convey the intangibility of nature and perception through stylization, the energy and vibrancy of the landscape here remain a subsidiary prop to the characters that form the focal point.

Finally, a discussion of this work should mention the discontinuity presented by the three mountaineers who traipse down across the picture plane. Disproportionately large and silhouetted against the snow, the three men prove a visual distraction, pulling the eye to a rather inconsequential moment that is, additionally, rendered rather simplistically. Bereft of either the skillful naturalism of the mountain characters or the liveliness of their surroundings, the crudely painted mountaineers seem out of place, an immature blemish on an otherwise well-crafted piece.

The second work, the mixed-media charcoal/watercolor drawing *Bergkulisse*, was one of the few mountain watercolors Nolde completed during his first stay in St. Gallen and dates to 1897, his final year in Switzerland. The most resounding effect of the work is the manner in which he begins to subordinate the composition to the color scheme. Rather than direct the viewer by means of its compositional elements, the painting progresses downward using "strong colour contrasts."[23] The radical shifts in temperature and luminosity across the broad swaths of color that trisect the painting's frame underlie the dynamism of the work. The three primary areas—the bright-orange twilit sky, the cool blue of the mountains, and the dark silhouette of the tree line below—divide the painting horizontally into nearly even thirds, with the creamy yellow reflection of the mountain lake at bottom offering a somewhat subtle rejoinder to this compositional simplicity.

When compared to *Jungfrau, Mönch und Eiger*, *Bergkulisse* seems, at first, to more closely approach the Expressionist style Nolde would soon embrace. Forms are reduced to colors and the atmosphere of the piece maintains a quiet reverence for the natural world. As Fluck notes, "although the watercolours were not yet freed from their purely descriptive function, the artist's desire to attain a more expansive, liberated deployment of this media is nevertheless clearly recognisable here."[24] Whatever Nolde gains from the compositional reduction that emphasizes these large blocks of color, however, he negates by the tenuousness of his brushstrokes and the emotional neutrality of the depiction. The calculated delineations between the different color regions—especially the careful outline of the mountains against the sky—sap the work of its potential energy (although they do also help to imbue the scene with a sense of depth). Additionally, the careful treatment of the subject matter mutes the action of the scene in a manner atypical of Nolde: as technically accomplished as the piece may be, the descriptive quality overbears his individual voice, verging on the decorative. Though the formal realism of the mountain postcards endures in this piece, Nolde seems to have lost some of the feeling and honesty that allowed the postcards to resonate with his audience in the first place.

Completed a half-century later, *Schweizer Berge* (*junge Frau im Vordergrund*)—a painting of his second wife, Jolanthe, on their honeymoon in 1948 (incidentally, Nolde's last trip to Switzerland)—clearly presents a radical creative departure from the above two pieces, capitalizing on Nolde's stylistic advancements to create a more vibrant and emotionally-nuanced piece. Playing across the page in a fit of apparent abstraction, the colors remain "constantly subject to the artist's creative will."[25] The rich, dark peak of the mountain—a brilliant wash of purple hues—holds the center of the image, embracing the form of its formlessness as it flows down from the top of the picture frame, "directly and inescapably [confronting] the viewer with [its] elemental force."[26] Curling into the purple of the mountainside, the more tangible, didactic clouds on the left balance the abstracted clouds that radiate off the right side of the peak—themselves little more than a bright white touched with a light yellow accent. While the purple of the peak pushes upward at points, pressing against the lighter hues that hold it from the clouds above, the softer blues of its base gently ground the mountain, with gradations in hue lending a sense of gravity and substance. The diagonals that repeat throughout the composition reinforce this downward, left-right movement across the frame.

The lines of blue that flow (or radiate from) Jolanthe retain a particular clarity amidst this movement of color, their swift strokes directing the eye of the viewer as they anchor themselves into her chest. And the young bride herself, a mere twenty-six years old to Nolde's eighty, holds the white of her form steadfast against the "color storm" that rages beyond. In her, the motion of the work finds a moment of concentration: her figure captures an instant of calm out of the action that abounds through the landscape, fixing and distilling the abandon out of which the mountain appears. A halo of warm tones accents the outline of her body, thrusting her into the foreground and asserting her presence amidst the cool hues of the mountainside. The subtler definitions of her features—the shadow cast by her hair, a bit of neckline above her blouse—also demonstrate a more intentioned treatment of her form. Such treatment, no doubt, speaks to the depth of feeling Nolde held for the young woman, though it conforms to a technique typical of his mountain watercolors. For Nolde, the inclusion of a figure often meant the opportunity for a counterpoint to the free color of the space: Fluck contends that "the particular attractiveness of these works results from the integration of the figures painted with a sovereign brushstroke into a complex, nearly abstract colour structure."[27] However, there is something distinctive about his treatment of Jolanthe. Whereas other of his watercolor figures offer abstractions of characters (a skier perhaps, or a climber), here he has created an individual. Her bowed head and articulated eye communicate a feeling of solemnity, almost mournfulness. Indeed, Nolde's journeys to the Alps had frequently provoked some nostalgia for his early years in St. Gallen: reflecting on his first return, he remarked how "what [he] saw when [he] was young had grown old. The city was certainly as lively as it ever was, but it all now seemed dead to [him]."[28] With this portrait of Jolanthe, he recognizes the inevitable onslaught of nature, its tendency towards destruction, but cannot help urging the preservation of the woman as she stands before him—perhaps a reflection on his own impending death and the knowledge that his new love would certainly outlive him.

Given that the most immediate ramification of the mountain postcards was to lay the groundwork for Nolde's future success, their role in his oeuvre seems rather utilitarian, their significance deriving less from their accomplishment as art-objects per se than from their accomplishment as lucrative art-commodities. However, one must recognize—as Nolde himself did—the persistence of the through lines that underlie his work: although the formal and stylistic tools he used clearly evolved, the content of his relationship with the landscape remained largely unchanged. Whether representing "a whole network of personified underworld forces, peeping out from behind their stony masks" or engaging in "an intimate collaboration between free forms in color and poetic figurations," he persistently sought to reveal the "mysterious, alluring reality [. . .] behind [the] visible [realm of] natural appearance."[29] For Nolde, the experience of the mountains was a revelation—one that he would mediate and retell in the art that he made there throughout his life.

## Notes

1. Paul Vogt, "Introduction," *Expressionism: A German Intuition, 1905–1920*, trans. Joachim Neugroschel (New York: Solomon R. Guggenheim Foundation, 1980), 22.

2. Peter Lasko, *The Expressionist roots of Modernism* (New York: Manchester University Press, 2003), 64;

Andrea Hollmann and Roland März, "Artists' Biographies," in *Arcadia and Metropolis: Masterworks of German Expressionism from the Nationalgalerie Berlin*, ed. Roland März (New York: Prestel, 2004), 152.

3. Hollmann and März, 152. Werner Haftmann, *Emil Nolde*, trans. Norbert Guterman (New York: Harry N. Abrams, 1959), 15; Martin Urban, "The North Germans: Paula Modersohn-Becker, Christian Rohlfs, Emil Nolde" in *Expressionism: A German Intuition, 1905–1920*, trans. Joachim Neugroschel (New York: Solomon R. Guggenheim Foundation, 1980), 35.

4. Andreas Fluck, "'Nature is delightful here and magnificent'—Nolde and Switzerland," in *Emil Nolde—Reiselust: Travels through Germany, Spain and Switzerland*, ed. Manfred Reuther, trans. Michael Wolfson (Cologne, Germany: Nolde Stiftung Seebüll and DuMont, 2010), 13.

5. Fluck, 15–16. Haftmann, 16. Vogt, 22.

6. Manfred Reuther, "'Greetings from our young garden'—Emil Nolde's Gardens and his Flower Paintings," in *Emil Nolde—My Garden full of Flowers*, ed. Manfred Reuther, trans. Michael Wolfson (Cologne, Germany: Nolde Stiftung Seebüll and DuMont, 2010), 17.

7. Fluck, 14.

8. Reuther, 17.

9. Fluck, 16.

10. Fluck, 16; Haftmann, 17.

11. Haftmann, 17; Lasko, 64; Fluck, 16.

12. Herbert, 21; Hollmann and März, 152.

13. Herbert, 21.

14. Urban, 35.

15. Hollmann and März, 152.

16. Urban, 34.

17. Fluck, 18.

18. Ibid., 18–19.

19. Ibid., 21.

20. Urban, 35.

21. Fluck, 16.

22. Ibid., 16.

23. Ibid., 16.

24. Ibid., 16.

25. Ibid., 19.

26. Ibid.

27. Ibid., 22.

28. Ibid., 18.

29. Haftmann., 10, 16, 35.


## Images

Emil Nolde, 1867-1956

*Jungfrau, Mönch und Eiger* (*Virgin, Monk and Eiger*) 1897

gouache, postcard, print, Mountain Postcards

8.8 x 13.6 cm (3.46 x 5.35 inches)

Stiftung Ada und Emil Nolde (Seebüll, Schleswig-Holstein, Germany)

Wesleyan University ARTstor ID 531360

http://library.artstor.org.ezproxy.wesleyan.edu/library/secure/ViewImages?id=4jEg
    cjQrIFhfKi83cVEXRn8mVHMidQ%3D%3D&userId=hzBH&zoomparams=

lso: http://www.harvardartmuseums.org/art/5309


Emil Nolde, 1867-1956

*Bergkulisse* (*Mountains*, or *Mountain Scenery*), Unpublished Cover Design for the
    Munich Magazine, *Jugend*, 1897

watercolor on paper, 39.5 x 29.2 cm (15.55 x 11.5 inches)

Stiftung Ada und Emil Nolde (Seebüll, Schleswig-Holstein, Germany)

Wesleyan University ARTstor ID 531362

http://library.artstor.org.ezproxy.wesleyan.edu/library/secure/ViewImages?id=4jEg
    cjQrIFhfKi83cVEXRn8mVHMheA%3D%3D&userId=hzBH&zoomparams=


Emil Nolde, 1867-1956

*Schweizer Berge* (*junge Frau im Vordergrund*) (*Swiss Mountains, Young Woman in
    Foreground*), 1848

*watercolor on paper,* 26.7 cm (10.51 in.), Width: 45.5 cm (17.91 in.)
Nolde Stiftung Seebüll (Germany—Neukirchen)
http://www.the-athenaeum.org/art/detail.php?ID=94905

# ARNOLD FANCK AND GERMAN *BERGFILM*

*Jackson Sabes*

Between 1921 and 1933, Dr. Arnold Fanck (1889–1974), a German geologist, mountaineer, and filmmaker, developed the film genre *"Bergfilm."* The *Bergfilm*, or mountain film, focused on the beauty of the German alpine landscape while using mountains as central elements to the story. Fanck's films brought to life the magnificent and awful power of the Alps. His films also served as effective propaganda tools for both Hannes Schneider's Arlberg downhill skiing technique and the spiritual restoration of Germany after the First World War. The German *Bergfilm* helped sensitize audiences to the transcendent nature and tangible sublimity of the Alpine landscape while popularizing a worldwide appreciation for speeding down the slopes on alpine skis.

While studying geology at the universities of Berlin and Munich, Fanck began to develop his skills in photography and mountaineering. After completing his doctorate in sedimentary geology, Fanck joined the German army in World War I as a photographic technician. With a strong background both as a mountaineer and as a cameraman, Fanck used his pay from his time in the army to purchase a camera and begin shooting.

It was through a chance meeting with the Austrian ski instructor Hannes Schneider that Fanck found his burgeoning studio, The Freiburg Mountain and Sports Film Company, its future star. Schneider was educated in skiing in Norway under Viktor Sohm in the winter of 1903–1904; he then returned to the Arlberg as a ski instructor. Over the next few winters, Schneider developed his own technique, utilizing the snowplow, the stem turn, and the stem-Christiania turns to create a new method that was both safe and fast.[1] Schneider used this technique to teach Austrian troops fighting on the Italian front during World War I, with much success. Upon his return from the war, Schneider's skiing technique became the subject of Franck's first film, the documentary *The Wonders of Skiing* (1920). The film was shot on the slopes of the Jungfrau and captured the perfect technique of Hannes Schneider.

Met with high acclaim, *The Wonders of Skiing* opened the door to more ski films shot by Fanck. *Struggle With the Mountain* (1921) premiered the next season, and Fanck was once again successful, both critically and financially. These two films created awareness for both Fanck's films and for the burgeoning sport of alpine skiing.[2] Due to the stranglehold on German film distribution by the UFA, Fanck and Schneider toured the films, showing them in rented theaters, tents, universities and ski clubs. The touring format proved successful, with each stop creating more devotees of Fanck's films and Schneider's skiing.

In 1923, Schneider's small ski school in St. Anton became so popular that he had to hire over 20 instructors to meet the demand. As popularity for Fanck's movies grew, so did the demand for Schneider both on camera and on the slopes. Schneider's fan base was largely responsible for the success that the films enjoyed. Fanck would later write about Schneider, "Without him, all my photographic knowledge would not have come to much."[3] It was the combination of these two expert mountaineers that made the quality of the films so high. The movies that Fanck and Schneider shot together were successful because of their authenticity. Fanck had precise control behind the camera and in the editing room and had an uncompromising desire to shoot on location. Schneider had an absolute mastery of his Arlberg technique and an ability to make skiing accessible and enjoyable. Fanck combined these attributes to make movies that captured not only people in the mountains, but the connection between people and those mountains as well.

In 1924, the Land Tyrol made Schneider's Arlberg technique the official technique for the entire region. In 1925, the Association of Tyrolean

Professional Ski Teachers and the Tyrolean Ski Association developed the first ski instructor's examination. In 1928, a law was passed that physical education teachers had to be not only skiers, but proficient teachers of Schneider's skiing system. Schneider was named the *Ehrenlehrrat*, honorary instructor, and *Ehrenförderer*, the honorary patron, of the German Ski Association.[4] The codification of ski instruction allowed the Arlberg technique to be easily exported around the world. Soon, Arlberg ski schools were built in London, France, and the United States, and skiing was taking the world by storm.

By 1928, there were enough expert skiers for a race between two large German ski clubs, the Arlberg club and the Kandahar club. The first race only had 45 entries and 300 spectators, but two years later, there were 140 men and 28 women with a crowd of 2000.[5] The race changed in 1934, though. Waiting on the racetrack of the Arlberg Kandahar Club, there was an ominous warning of the future for both skiing and Fanck's films. At the end of the last race of the Land Tyrol championships, "*Deutschland über Alles*" came ringing out from Nazis in the crowd, and "*Sieg Heil*" overtook the traditional skiing greeting of "*Ski Heil*" as the Nazis began to salute. Nazi hooliganism had overtaken the ski course. The Austrians had to end many races that season due to Nazi disruptions, but soon, it would be more than ski races that were disrupted by the Nazis.

Fanck and Schneider would make several more films together, most notably *Der Heilige Berg* (1926), *The White Hell of Piz Palü* (1928), and *White Ecstasy* (1931). Fanck's films were very well received across Germany, winning acclaim from both the political left and the nationalistic sectors. *Der Heilige Berg* was lauded by the Social Democratic *Vorwärts* magazine, saying that the film "impart[s] to millions, both in Germany and throughout the entire world, visual delight and a heightened feeling for nature's vast and demonic powers."[6] The Communist Party's publication *Die Rote Fahne* said that *The White Hell of Piz Palü* was "undoubtedly one of the best German films ever,"[7] and also wrote of *Avalanche*, "the director was able to visualize the power of nature (without any idyllic razzle-dazzle in its treatment of nature) in constantly changing, stirring images."[8] Abroad, Fanck's films were praised for the profound resonance of his imagery. In 1937 the *Hartford Courant* reviewed Fanck's *White Ecstasy* (then known as *Ski Chase*) saying, "Until you have seen 'Ski Chase', you really don't know what the word skiing means."[9] Fanck's films became the standard for what a movie about the mountains should look like. Fanck captured, on camera, the very meaning of the word skiing—not just groups of Tyroleans cruising down a hill. Fanck captured the speed, the danger, and the grace of skiing on film.

As Fanck's renown grew, so did his cast. His films evolved from documentary efforts shooting Schneider skiing in the Einegade to large-scale melodramas with recurring casts and crews seeking to continually pioneer skiing and the *Bergfilm*. Fanck's cadre was one of the reasons for his great success. His productions continuously employed Sepp Allgeier as a cameraman. Allgeier was an important aid to Fanck, thanks to his high level of experience as a mountaineer, as a cameraman, and as an expert Schwarzwald skier. Fanck also went on to hire other cinematographers, including the aptly named Hans Schneeberger, Albert Benitz, Richard Angst, and Walter Riml. These cameramen working under Fanck's tutelage made up a generation of filmmakers that left a large impact on German film throughout the 1950s.[10] Fanck's cameramen developed skills and techniques to meet Fanck's heavy demands on them. The skills learned under Fanck kept many aspects of the *Bergfilm* alive in German cinema, including when Sepp Allgeier created the same powerful visuals of Fanck's films as the photographic director of *Triumph of the Will*.

Fanck's two most famous protégés were Luis Trenker and Leni Riefenstahl. Trenker was a top skier in Schneider's Arlberg school, and would go on to make Bergfilms of his own. Riefenstahl would also make films after working for Fanck—most notably the notorious propaganda film of the Third Reich, *The Triumph of the Will*. Riefenstahl became the leading woman in many of Fanck's films, and she became a capable skier herself under the guidance of Trenker and Walter Pager.[11] Fanck's protégés kept his pedigree alive, Trenker becoming a symbol of the Alps and Riefenstahl creating powerful visuals meant to inspire in another realm.

Fanck's expansion wasn't limited to the size of his cast. Throughout his career, he developed a large suite of technical abilities. He began shooting from skis, shooting on slope, shooting in all weather conditions, and, most notably, shooting with a slow motion camera. Fanck's films took on the challenge of capturing these difficult shots on the mountain instead of a soundstage, making no concessions to convenience over authenticity. Fanck developed these skills to make movies of mountains, not movies that only had mountains in them. He sought to take his camera deep into the backcountry so that the mountains could provide just as much of a backdrop to the narrative as the narrative was a backdrop to the mountains.

One of Fanck's most famous techniques was the slow motion camera. The slow motion camera was developed during the Great War in order to measure the curve and mass of a projectile, and as an impressionable young camera technician for the German army, Fanck was left in awe of its effect.[12] When Fanck recalled the power of seeing slow motion footage during the war, he said, "the memory, of a shell as if it were floating in the air . . . boring itself leisurely, as it were, before my eyes through the think armor-plating never left me." Shooting Fanck's films themselves was a feat of mountaineering. The camera Fanck's team carried up the mountains weighed in at over 1100 pounds and was hauled up 3000 meters for shooting.[13] Fanck would pull the camera behind a team of horses so that he could capture slow motion shots of Hannes Schneider jumping cliffs and racing down mountains. Fanck's new techniques helped to create sublime and moving images of the Alps and to highlight the action filled ski chases of Schneider. In the 1920s, before skiing and slow motion were commonplace, the slowed cliff jumps of Schneider left lasting impressions on audiences similar to Fanck watching the slow motion shell in midair.

Critics responded well to Fanck's approach to his films. His efforts were rewarded with memorable images that captured audiences. In a review of *Avalanche*, the German newspaper *Lichtbild-Bühne* regarded the movie as:

An exciting evening. Surmounting the peaks of Europe . . . the peaks of cinematic art. Only an exhilaration which takes people to the outer limits of human capacity can manage to stir our entire being in such a manner.[14]

In the same way the audience didn't know what skiing was until they saw *The White Ecstasy*, the audience did not know the Alps until they saw Fanck's work.

Fanck's work imbued the Alps with mystical transcendent powers. His method of filming did not diminish the Alps into kitsch representations but instead simulated the same experience mountain climbers faced there. Fanck's mountains were dangerous and vast, dwarfing the size of humans on screen. They were powerful and filled the entire frame. For Fanck's hero, either climbing the mountains or skiing down them was a dangerous journey.

Fanck was able to create such powerful images of mountains through different film techniques. In Eric Rentschler's essay, "Relocating the Bergfilm," he writes that Fanck was able to evoke "the impetus of artists like Caspar David Friedrich, Phillip Otto Runge, and Joseph Anton Koch" as familiar motif sets to the German people in order to inspire an atmosphere of sublimity.[15] Retschler goes on to emphasize that Fanck wouldn't diminish his mountains in their magnitude and massive proportions—instead, the only points of comparison in the *mise-en-scene* of the film's clouds and mountains are the miniscule humans interacting with these massive elements.[16] This atmosphere of sublimity displayed the power of the mountains and made audiences receptive to the transcendental nature of the mountains.

In his essay, Rentschler regards Fanck as "an adversary of Hollywood's linearity and 'tempo,' a filmmaker whose aesthetics accorded preeminence to contemplation and meditation [who] recognized the inevitability of narrative concessions."[17] Fanck wasn't creating Nazi imagery to rearm a German public. His goal was to create visual spectacle within the high mountains. Fanck's films shift focus from narrative to actually characterizing the Alps that surround the camera.

Rentschler points out that Ernst Bloch's 1909 essay "The Alps Without Photography" foreshadows this understanding. Bloch concludes his essay by saying, "it is not without reason that a quietly beautiful wooden fountain on a village lane in Garmisch harmonizes so well—with such a sense of auratic revelation—with the alpine peaks beyond: as though their positions were reversible, allowing each to serve as the other's background."[18] The source of Fanck's excellence lies in his ability to create alpine atmospherics that can also be the main focus of the film simultaneously.

Skiing and Fanck's films reached extremely high levels of popularity during the Weimar Republic because they were a result of the First World

War, as well as a cure for the postwar plagues of Germany. In Wilfried Wilms's essay "The Essence of the Alpine World is Struggle," Wilms speculates that the German *Bergfilm* is a product of the experience of invisibility and trauma after the loss of the First World War. Wilms believed that the early *Bergfilm* was an aesthetic vehicle to help cope with the trauma of Germany's defeat.[19] With three million men dead, and 4.2 million men returning wounded and disgraced by defeat, the Weimar consciousness was consumed in shame, humiliation, emasculation, and embarrassment over the end of the Wilhelmine Empire.

In the wake of the war, the Alps and the *Bergfilm* offered themselves as a way to return to German strength and heroism. Skiing allowed Germans to leave their broken urban lives, which lacked purpose and meaning, to enter the alpine world, full of heroism and sublime adventure. By inspiring the men and women of Germany to leave the plagues of postwar Germany for the struggles of snow, ice, and rock, Fanck's films had a prescriptive element to help restore the nation.

Fanck's films acted as an antidote for the postwar plagues of Germany. The *Bergfilm* was unique thanks to its ability to elevate the German national psyche and elevate it to the same heights as the great peaks the films captured by showing viewers the power and majesty of their native land. The *Bergfilm* took images from the peaks and carried them back into the valley to show the view from above. But did these films inspire viewers to heal and recover with the living rock companions Fanck's films created, or was it propaganda meant to remilitarize the German Aryan culture?

Skiing itself had already been under siege. Mussolini ordered a road to be built to the mountain ski resort of Terminillo, and began offering it as a *Dopolavoro* excursion for Italian city folk.[20] Sestrières became the first Italian ski resort in the Alps, meant to be a "triumph of the most up-to-date technical rationalization applied to the organization of a skiing center."[21] Sestrières had 74 runs, twenty of which required no climbing whatsoever thanks to mechanized lifts, along with two cable cars servicing the mountain. Meanwhile, elsewhere in central Europe, anti-Semitism had poisoned the ski clubs of Austria and Germany, which required members to have Aryan heritage to join.[22]

Even the world's top skier wasn't spared from the purging of Alpine skiing. Schneider was jailed during the *Anchluss* in 1938. Schneider was called a "ravenous Jew" and a "devourer of Nazis" by the German *Schwarze Korps* and *Der Rote Adler*. Schneider was jailed as a capitalistic exploiter of the German people and a Jewish sympathizer. Leni Riefenstahl, Schneider's old co-star in Fanck films who had since risen to fame in the Third Reich, was spitefully pleased with his jailing.[23] Schneider was eventually freed from prison with the help of Dr. Karl Rösen who had been Hitler's counsel after the Beerhall Putsch.

Schneider moved to the United States on February 9, 1939 to help run the North Conway ski resort in New Hampshire. His jailing shows that the Nazi Party's aims and the aims of Fanck were not in line. While Fanck eventually became a member of the Nazi Party to maintain his filmmaking career, Schneider's jailing and his relocation to the United States suggest that the Arlberg technique and downhill skiing could not be totally appropriated or controlled by the Nazis as a method of remilitarizing Germans.

Fanck offered his audiences a new sensitivity to the alpine landscapes featured in his films and helped the audience to replicate the experience of sublimity and transcendence that dwells in the peaks. For a country torn apart by war, ravaged by inflation, and embarrassed by defeat, these were prescriptive elements for recovery. For the thousands of viewers who saw Fanck's films, the movies were effective propaganda for the Arlberg school and alpine skiing. For anyone who sees them, even today, they persist as powerful documentary efforts that chronicle the beauty of the high mountains. In the end, Fanck's films don't persist for their political messages. They last because they are beautiful images of incredible places. They are souvenirs taken from the heavens that few men and women will ever reach. They are trail maps carried from the peaks down to the valley dwellers below so that we, too, may ascend to those great heights and ski down them. Fast.

## Notes

1. John B. Allen, *Culture and Sport of Skiing* (Amherst: University of Massachusetts Press, 2007), 261.

2. Michelle Langford, ed. "Film Pioneers, Arnold Fanck," *Directory of World Cinema: Germany*, Vol. 10 (Bristol: Intellect Books, 2012), 19.

3. Arnold Fanck, "Er Führte Regie mit Gletschern," *Allgemeine Sport-Zeitung,* (22 March 1914) 90–93.

4. E. John B. Allen, *The Culture and Sport of Skiing: From Antiquity to World War II* (Amherst: University of Massachusetts Press, 2007), 264.

5. Allen, 265.

6. Eric Rentschler, "Mountains and Modernity," *Vorwärts* (19 December 1926), 143.

7. ibid.

8. ibid.

9. "Ski Chase,' Film Show At Avery, Thrilling Picture," *Hartford Courant,* 31 Jan 1937: C7.

10. Rentschler, 141.

11. Allen, 262.

12. Allen, 264.

13. Fanck, *Er Führte Regie mit Gletschern* (Nymphenburger Verlagshandlung, 1973), 115.

14. Review, *Lichtbild-Bühne,* 3 February 1931. In Klaus Kreimeier and Stiftung Deutsche Kinemathek,

*Fanck—Trenker—Riefenstahl: der deutsche Berg film und seine Folgen* (Berlin, 1972), E3.

15. Rentschler, 147.

16. ibid.

17. Rentschler, 142.

18. Ernst Bloch, "The Alps Without Photography," *Literary Essays,* trans. Andrew Joran (Stanford University Press, 1998) P. 441.

19. Wilfried Wilms, "The Essence of the Alpine World is Struggle"—Strategies of Gesundung in Arnold Fanck's Early Mountain Films," in *Heights of Reflection: Mountains in the German Imagination from the Middle Ages to Present,* eds. Caroline Schaumann and Sean Ireton. (Camden House 2012), 269.

20. Allen, 243.

21. Guido Tonella, *Skiing at Sestrières,* trans. Katherine Natzio (Sestrières: Movemento del Sestrières, 1934), 13.

22. Allen, 246.

23. Friedl Pfeifer and Morten Lund, "The Making of the Aspen Dream," TMS, 49, 124.

# THIS WILD COUNTRY: JACK KEROUAC'S *THE DHARMA BUMS* AND THE MOUNTAINS[1]

*Catherine Walsh*

It's a common adolescent fantasy: to pack up your things and run away from home, away from all the responsibility and heartache of growing up. It's about escaping from all the entanglements of everyday society and pushing back against the encroaching mediocrity of adult life. It doesn't matter where you go to seek an alternative, but you might as well go into the mountains, those eternal, solemn, desperate places that have for thousands of years housed hermits, monks, and madmen looking for truth. Jack Kerouac (1922–1969) taps into the fantasy of running away to find ourselves in several of his books, and deals specifically with mountains and mountain-climbing in his mostly autobiographical work *The Dharma Bums,* completed in 1958. In this novel, Ray Smith, a character generally acknowledged to be a thinly disguised stand-in for Kerouac himself, travels the United States and Mexico on foot, by bus, and in the cars of strangers as a hitchhiker, calling himself a "Dharma Bum," or "religious wanderer," with reference to the Buddhist doctrine and truth.[2] He climbs the Californian Matterhorn peak and spends a summer as a fire lookout atop Desolation Peak in Washington. These experiences frame the events of the novel and connect Kerouac's wanderlust to the American landscape and the spirituality of the mountains. In *The Dharma Bums,* the mountains tempt those who wish to escape society into the persistent, childlike dream of the wilderness, and reward worthy ascendants with unmatched spiritual exuberance.

Before ascending into the higher terrain of Kerouac's novel, however, one ought to note the layers of spirituality in his past. Han Shan's Cold Mountain Poems inclined Kerouac's still-developing Buddhist beliefs towards solitary meditation. Kerouac was raised in a Catholic family, but began to study Buddhism in earnest late in 1953. Upon meeting a translator of Han Shan's poetry, Gary Snyder (b. 1930), who appears in *The Dharma Bums* under the name Japhy Ryder, Kerouac is "overjoyed."[3] Snyder's work centered on the poetry Han Shan produced while living in withdrawn solitude at Cold Mountain in China and conducting a "spiritual search." Naturally the freedom and the isolation enshrined in Han Shan's work appealed to Kerouac, the perennial countercultural drifter. Kerouac presents Han Shan's poems, as translated by Japhy, as the impetus for Smith's journey into the mountains. The novel begins and ends with the poetry of Han Shan, and is even dedicated to the poet, so it is worth examining his effect on Kerouac. In *The Dharma Bums*, Kerouac "stresses Han Shan's loner status while touching sparingly on Han Shan's reclusive life and Buddhist ideas."[4] Kerouac sees Han Shan as a wanderer outside of society similar to himself and his friends in the Beat generation, and so jumps at the opportunity to follow in his footsteps and climb a mountain when Japhy offers to guide him up the Matterhorn.

The character of Japhy Ryder becomes identified with Han Shan himself as a kind of "dual hero" of both Eastern philosophy and American optimism. Japhy dresses differently even from other intellectual poets in his circle, in "rough workingman's clothes . . . to serve him on mountain climbs and hikes."[5] He wants to give the impression that vanity is not part of his psyche. His eyes "twinkled like the eyes of old giggling sages of China," and he "opened his mouth wide to guffaw at jokes."[6] He is identified with laughter and wise men at the same time, with China and with "oldtime lumberjacks."[7]

In *The Dharma Bums*, as in the poetry of Han Shan, the wilderness is valorized as a place entirely free of modern civilization. Japhy objects to camping in a meadow partway up the Matterhorn on the grounds that he and Smith "could wake up tomorrow morning and find three dozen schoolteachers on horseback frying bacon."[8] The impulse to scale often-treacherous mountainsides comes from a desire to escape other human beings and be in solitude. At the higher camp Japhy wants to reach, there "won't be one human being."[9] The novel presents this solitude as the ideal, the sublime, and the goal of all the mountain goat adventures the Dharma Bums embark on. Japhy characterizes Han Shan, the novel's underpinning hero, as someone who "got sick of the big city and the world and took off to hide in the mountains."[10] The mountains provide an escape. These early reflections on the solitude offered by the wilderness have an airy idealism to them: the representatives of society are schoolteachers and an abstract city.

The immediate danger of immoral civilization takes frightening shape later on when Smith reaches Mexico over the course of an alcohol and marijuana-fueled night during which a gay Mexican boy falls for Smith. It is this experience that leads Smith to call the city "evil" and the desert "virtuous."[11] The city symbolizes excess in food, drink, and sex, and the desert represents aestheticism and spiritual enlightenment. Faced with another party at a cottage of one of the Beat poets, Smith remarks to himself: "sociability is just a big smile and a big smile is nothing but teeth"[12] The power of Smith's dark reflection lies in its inherent menace: teeth imply animal violence and the possibility of being physically chewed up by having to be sociable.

The novel's structure of characters and encounters divides middle class Americans and the lunatic "Dharma Bums." In Smith's nomadic life, there are few consistent characters who do not also subscribe to some form of counterculturalism. His encounters with "conventional" (i.e., settled, non-nomadic) men and women, or, on occasion, truckers are brief, superficial affairs with waitresses and truck drivers: representatives of modern American middle-class society. These people often conclude that Smith and his friends are "hopeless eccentrics."[13] Again and again, Smith runs up against expectations of behavior for a young man: a "nice woman" in a diner in Bridgeport, CA asks if he and his friends are going hunting, and when he replies that they intend to climb Matterhorn, she says she "wouldn't do that if somebody paid [her] a thousand dollars!"[14] He imagines his mother worrying over him, thinking "why isn't he like other men?"[15] Part of the appeal and mystique of becoming a *bhikku*, or Buddhist wandering monk, lies in the assertion of one's individuality endemic to giving up what is commonly assumed to be desirable. Leaving mainstream society, however, did not mean that self-imposed exiles like Smith and Japhy were without a community of their own. Even in the North Cascades, a "community of lookouts" chats over two-way radios from the summits of their respective mountains.[16] The mountains breed camaraderie between those who have chosen to take refuge there.

One recurring character, Henry Morley, though a figure in Beat poet circles, nevertheless does not lose his identification with a class of scholars and as such does not achieve transcendent joy in mountain climbing. Morley betrays his attitude towards the mountains in the "huge amounts of junk he want[s] to take on the climb," including a rubber air mattress.[17] His manner of speaking is "incomprehensible," rendered in the text with little punctuation and rapid changes of topic within the same sentence.[18] Smith describes him as looking "funny . . . just like he does in the library" as they set out on their hike: Morley is a disciple of book learning.[19] He is out of his element in the mountains. Morley falls even further in the esteem of Japhy and Smith when he uses the mountain call "Yodelayhee" "at the oddest moments and in oddest circumstances," reflecting his disconnect from his surroundings.[20] Japhy replaces the European alpine call "Yodelayhee" with a "simple 'Hoo' which he said was the Indian way to call in the mountains."[21] Morley tries to apply knowledge to the mountains which is not native to them. Japhy and Smith are in some profound way American—they want to be like the Indians, the original landholders, with their direct relationship to the land they live on. Japhy imitates "the Indians" often in the wilderness, especially with his habit of climbing mountains naked. Morley, then, with his Eurocentrism, with his "collection of snow covered mountain photos" from an Alpine trek, is the antithesis of these two.[22] Rather than look at the American peak before him, he mentions photos he has of an Alpine peak. He is profoundly disconnected. Morley's realization that "he'd forgotten to drain the crankcase" of his car when they are already four miles into their hike and his subsequent solitary haul back down the mountain reveals his ties to that suburban world of cars and comfort.[23] He has more in common with the people who pick up hitchhikers like Smith than such carefree wanderers as Smith himself.

The threat of middle-class American suburbia, with its carefully ordered homogeneity, compels Smith and his nonconformist friends to the chaotic wilderness of the mountains. Smith imagines walking down a "suburban street" with "house after house on both sides of the street" and describes the scene within all of them. Everything is the same: the "lamplight of the living room," the "little blue square of the television," the family watching "probably one show." The homogeneity of the suburban street is anathema to Smith: he seeks his own individuality in the mountains, far from the conformity of the suburbs. The "blue television windows of homes" are as much a part of their architecture as their literal windows. Physically outside the space of the homes, "alone, his thoughts the only thoughts not electrified to the Master Switch," Japhy "stalk[s]" along. Dogs bark at him because he "pass[es] on human feet instead of on wheels."[24]

The alienation and loneliness of this vision are the cost of freedom from suburban conformity, the cost of reclaiming individual humanity from the indistinguishable homes of the town. When Japhy's sister Rhoda comes to visit him in the days before her marriage to her "well-dressed" fiancé, Japhy exclaims in anger and hurt: "What you wanta get all involved in the middle class for, Rhoda?"[25] Japhy stands solidly outside this world of marriage and comfort, living instead in his own land of free love and quasi-religious poverty. He is a latter-day hermit. He will remain outside the suburban homes. His sister will live inside. Here in Japhy's sense of betrayal we see the consequences of leaving society behind.

The motif of dreams, often in connection with wild landscapes, reveals the connection between the wilderness and man's subconscious. When one is alone in nature, it is easy to imagine that the mountains exist only for oneself, and perhaps only as a figment of one's imagination. Our experiences of the mountains reflect our relationships with them: thus, a safe and pleasant place to camp becomes an "incomparable dreamy meadow."[26] While a mountain meadow might be dreamlike, a climbing experience can just as easily turn frightening and nightmarish; Kerouac does not hide the difficulty of scaling rough mountain peaks. Coming back down the Matterhorn, "as in a happy dream, with the suddenness of waking up from an endless nightmare," Smith and friends reach the bottom of the trail.[27] Here leaving the mountain after he has scaled it is a relief, and the mountain is the nightmare: how we are feeling, physically and emotionally, about a trail affects how we perceive it. This idea of a fluid, changeable perception of reality dovetails nicely with Japhy's Buddhist assertion that everything exists only in the mind: all is "completely serious, all completely halluci-nated, all completely happy."[28]

Smith and his fellow Dharma Bums shirk conventional responsibility in favor of a life of travel and unaccountability, thus acting out a desire to never grow up into adult life. As he comes down the mountains, Smith compares his exhaustion to that of a "little boy" who has "spent a whole day rambling alone in the woods and fields," to "little Indian boys" and "little Arab boys" following their fathers, and to "a little girl pulling her lit-tle brother home on the sled."[29] The repetition of the word "little" reflects the sense that one has in the mountains of being dwarfed by the grandeur of nature, the sheer size of the surrounding formations of earth. The irre-sponsibility and simple joy of spending a whole day in the woods before you must "put on a straight face again for the world of seriousness" has very much in common with childhood freedom.[30] Smith sees himself not only as like a little child, but like all little children everywhere: the desire to be away from the "world of seriousness" in the mountains is to his mind universal and identified with youth, as evidenced by his inclusion of "In-dian" and "Arab" boys.

Again and again the mountains act as a passageway through which one may return to childhood simplicity. Upon reaching the Desolation Peak lookout, Smith feels "happier than . . . since childhood," and as he de-scribes his craving for a Hershey bar to Japhy, the two "talk like two chil-dren." Smith on returning to civilization after climbing Matterhorn wakes up "like a little child and [is] told he [is] home."[31] From these examples we can deduce that for Smith, the mountains and especially the feeling of returning from the mountains are identified with childhood and the escape from adult society. At last, Smith's childishness allows him to reach tran-scendence: after essentially throwing a temper tantrum where he "throws himself right on the ground and crie[s]," he experiences "the tender bliss of enlightenment . . . like milk in [his] eyelids."[32] His emotional, childlike state is the prerequisite of the "milk" of enlightenment—and significantly, he refers to it as milk, as the soothing antidote to his childish tears.

Smith and Japhy's exuberant wonder at the mountains emphasizes a simple, instinctual creativity reminiscent of childhood, marked especially by their use of neologisms and the language of color. Describing dusk falling on the mountains, Smith mentions the "pinkening deepening blue sky" and later on the same day the "graying" of early evening.[33] The energetic creation of new words and the use of the progressive tense lends a living immediacy of color and motion to the scene. Han Shan's poems were "never canonized"[34] into the Chinese tradition because of their scorn for traditional poetic structure and devices; likewise, Japhy and Smith make up haikus "without literary devices or fanciness of expression" in an effort to convey a more direct and unmediated experience of the natural world.[35] As a result, Kerouac's writing on the mountains is constantly fresh and genuine-feeling, with such evocative descriptions as a place "suddenly gladey and dark with shade and a tremendous cataracting stream . . . bashing and frothing over scummy rocks and tumbling on down."[36] By writing long sentences and using polysyndeton, or the proliferation of conjunctions, especially "and," Kerouac successfully conveys the verve one might feel in the mountain landscape.

A second component of the mountain experience as told by Kerouac is a free, immediate, direct spirituality conveyed by his energetic descriptions of his (or Smith's) surroundings. Smith and Japhy meditate in the mountains in pursuit of enlightenment; Smith feels that "the mountains [are] indeed Buddhas and [their] friends" and easily applies Buddhist sayings such as "when you get to the top of a mountain, keep climbing" to his literal world.[37] Kerouac wildly fuses American and Eastern beliefs, as he trusts in the natural world around him. As Japhy and Smith leap down the mountain, Smith compares their improvisational movement downhill both to jazz and to the motions of Chinese lunatics in one long exuberant paragraph.[38] Japhy says, "the closer you get to real matter, rock air fire and wood, boy, the more spiritual the world is."[39] This seemingly self-contradictory belief is what guides Japhy and Smith into the mountains: only by getting in touch with the physical word of matter, nature, and the elements can they experience the kind of spiritual transcendence they seek. As Smith walks along the trail, its "immortal look" leads him to meditate on his own past lives, the "golden eternities of past childhood or past manhood" and even to feel "ecstasy."[40] Smith, and Kerouac, see the mountain landscape as a meditation object. The timelessness of the natural world, the sensation one gets that a mountain has been where it is forever and will remain there for thousands of years, facilitates recognition of one's own past lives.

*The Dharma Bums* appeals to generation after generation of American Buddhists, mountaineers, hitchhikers, dreamers, and all those who do not want to grow up. I read this book for the first time this summer, the copy I held marked with the annotations of seven previous readers, some of whom I know well, and others I have never met. I read it alone by the side of a lake, or on a sailboat in the middle of the water, or on a train. Yet I was never really alone—in the margins, in crabbed handwriting and in tiny absentminded doodles on the pages, fellow seekers on the cusp of adulthood followed me through the book like raggedy ghosts. Kerouac's novel is not without problems: the women in the book, for example, rarely have any place among the company of outcasts except as sexual objects for the men. Yet despite its flaws, the book's wilderness writing captures the sheer exuberance and spirituality one feels when in close contact with nature. Even the occasional sloppy or lazy metaphor adds to the charm of *The Dharma Bums*: of course Kerouac would go for the near-at-hand image, as he is making up his poetry as he goes along. Though I am no dharma bum myself, I have met several people who could not be accurately categorized under any other name; it is because of them that I think so highly of travelling the mountains.

## Notes

1. Jack Kerouac, *The Dharma Bums* (New York: The Viking Press, 1958).

2. Kerouac, 5.

3. Ling Chung, "Han Shan, Dharma Bums, and Charles Frazier's Cold Mountain," *Comparative Literature Studies* 48 (2011): 547. Also see: Gary Snyder, *Cold Mountain Poems* (Berkeley: Counterpoint; Har/Com edition 2013).

4. Chung, 549.

5. Kerouac, 11.

6. Ibid.

7. Ibid.

8. Ibid., 63.

9. Ibid.

10. Ibid., 20.

11. Ibid., 156.

12. Ibid., 192.

13. Ibid., 47.

14. Ibid., 51.

15. Ibid., 132.

16. Ibid., 168.

17. Ibid., 40.

18. Ibid., 40.

19. Ibid., 56.

20. Ibid., 49.

21. Ibid., 50.

22. Ibid., 51.

23. Ibid., 56.

24. Ibid., 104.

25. Ibid., 185.

26. Ibid., 62.

27. Ibid., 91.

28. Ibid., 71.

29. Ibid., 88.

30. Ibid., 88.

31. Ibid., 236, 212, 93.

32. Ibid., 136–137.

33. Ibid., 87.

34. Chung, "Han Shan," 543.

35. Kerouac, 59.

36. Ibid., 60.

37. Ibid., 70.

38. Ibid., 85.

39. Ibid., 206.

40. Ibid., 61–62.

# KING ORTLER; CLIMBING AS EXPERIENCE, A PHOTO ESSAY

*Peter Mark*

August 22, 2015

The early morning sun touches the peaks above the village of Sulden. From our terrace the broad green valley lies in half-light, dark green wedges of forest rising to the pale rounded lower hills. Behind and above loom the grey battlements, flecked with white, of limestone cliffs. High, impossibly high above everything, shining pure white against the azure sky, soars the summit ridge of the Ortler.

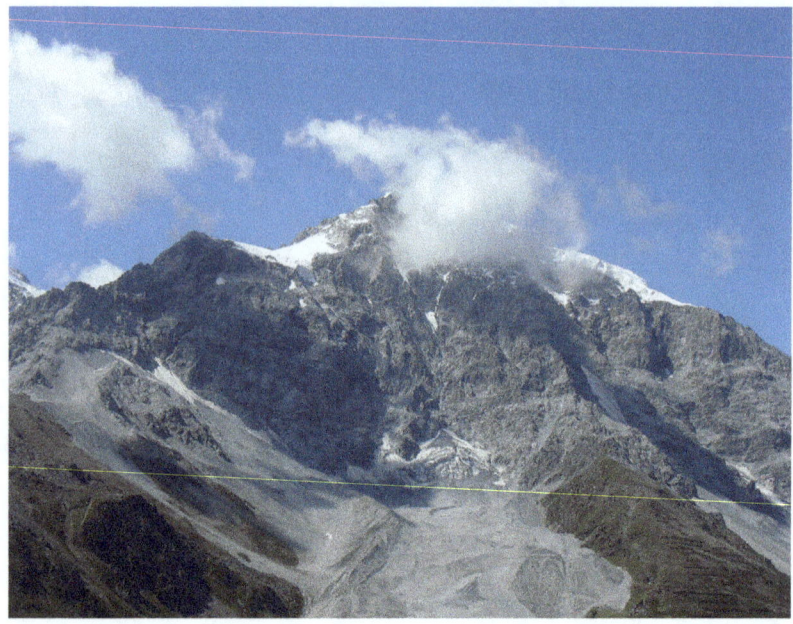

"King Ortler." The first time I saw its majestic white crown, high above the village of Trafoi in the German-speaking Sudtirol, I knew I must try to climb it. Five years later, I have achieved this goal.

Last night, looking up from Sulden, it was difficult to imagine, *This morning I was up there.* The Ortler is technically the most difficult and psychologically certainly the most demanding climb I have ever attempted. The combination of rock climbing and steep glacier, of altitude and cold, requires a continuous high level of concentration from the moment one leaves the Payer Hütte, perched on a rock *arête* at 10,000 feet, to the time one returns. Even the two-hour hike up to the hut, the last 45 minutes along a steep and narrow trail, followed by a rock crest where one is secured by a cable anchored to the rock (a *via ferrata*), was close to terrifying. Such a narrow and vertiginous way, with a thousand meters of air beneath my feet, frightens me more than the technical climbing that comes later. I had to face my personal terror—I nearly called off the climb—and face it alone. Amidst the mist and the immensity of space and of broken rocks, the feeling of solitude is overwhelming. Here is the "Sublime" of which Ruskin and Emerson speak.

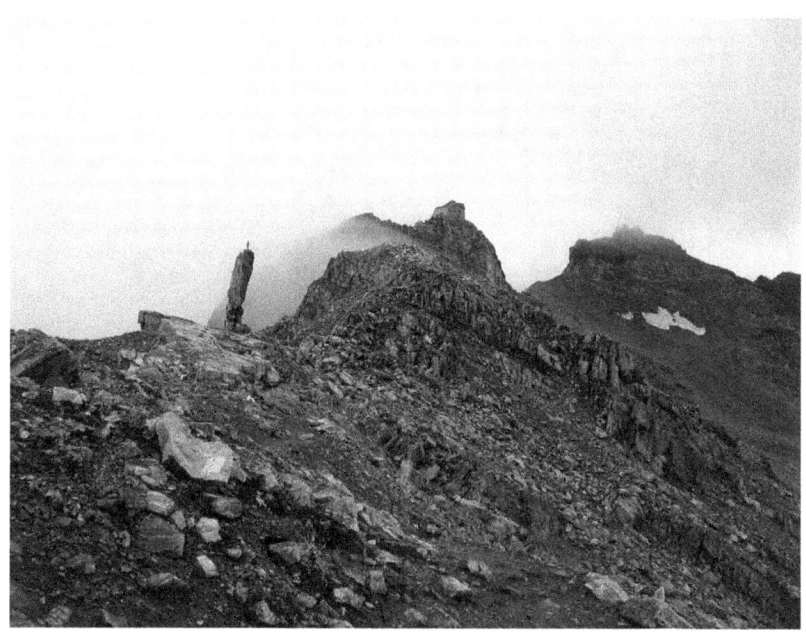

The Julius Payer Hut is named for an Austrian military officer, climber, polar explorer, artist. The narrow, tall structure sits on a rock promontory. How it was built, at the end of the 19th century, I cannot imagine. Accommodations are simple: Two W.C.s for 50 guests, one source of running water, which is not potable. The dining room was crowded with 40 other climbers when I arrived at 6:30 p.m. Though "lights out" is at 10, the night was short. Gerd Schönthaler, my guide and friend, met me at the hut at 8:30, and we were up at 3:50 a.m. A few slices of white bread and butter and a cup of black coffee and then we roped up—*before* we left the terrace of the hut—at 4:50 a.m.

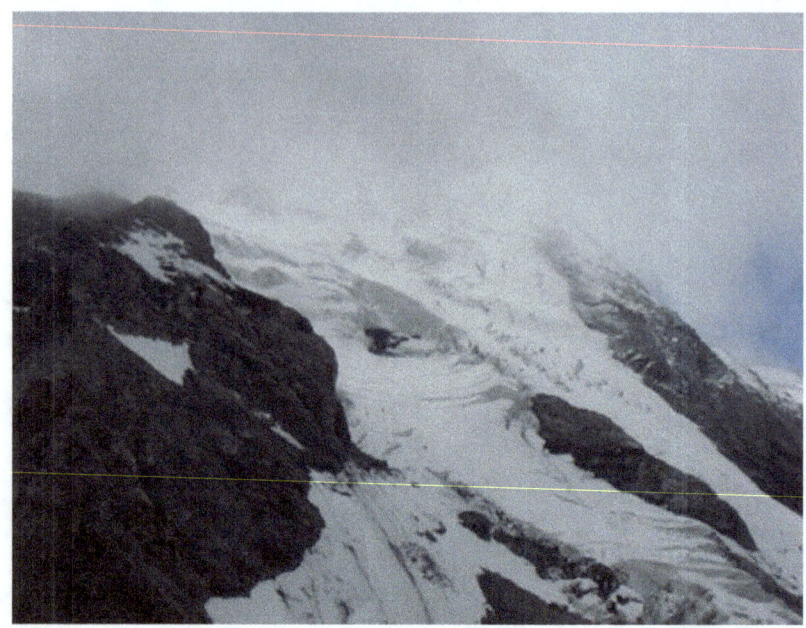

For the first hour, we were rock climbing in pitch blackness, our route illuminated only by our headlamps; all we could see was the rock immediately in front of us, which helps one's concentration marvelously. Steep pitches of cliff face were interspersed with short stretches along the narrow rock crest or *Grat*. At one moment, in the darkness, I noticed a light to my left. I looked down . . . and realized the light I saw was actually the lights of Sulden, 1,500 meters straight down. I looked to the right . . . and there were lights from Trafoi, 1,700 meters down. Like flying but without the airplane. I tried to look straight ahead.

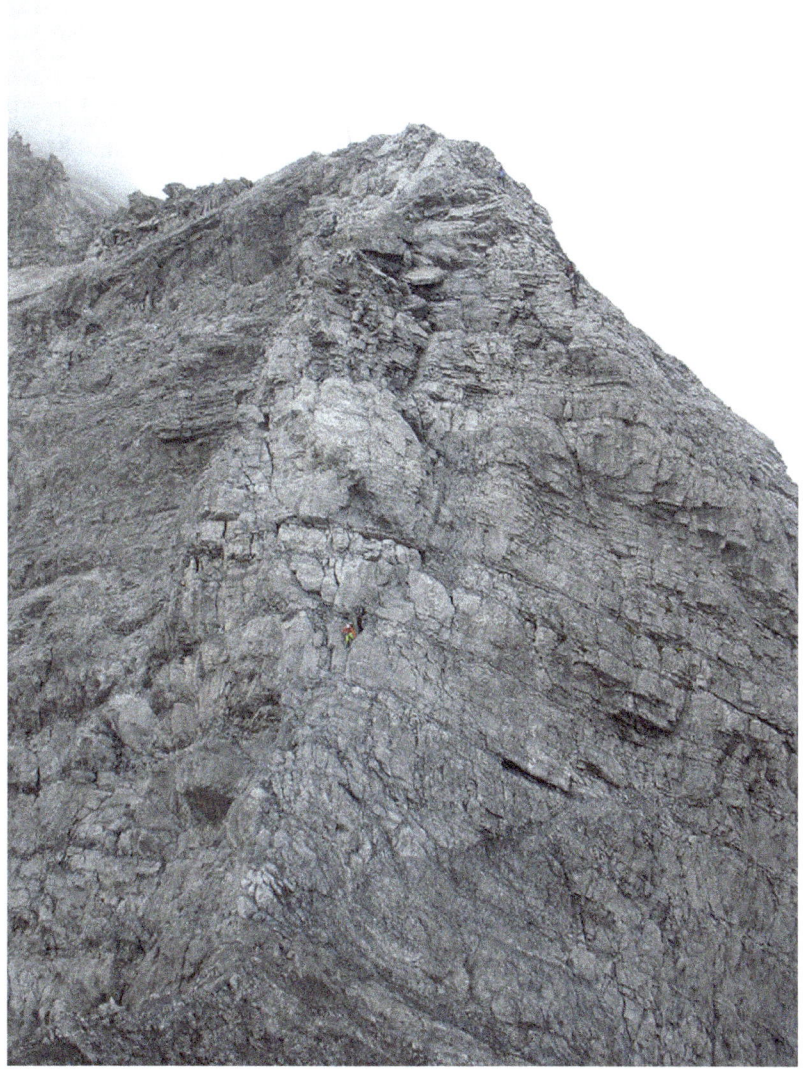

With fixed cables on the steepest pitches for security, and with Gerd's reassuring belay, I truly enjoy rock climbing. Gerd conveys a feeling of confidence. When I climb with him, I am a decent rock climber. Climbing alone, I have on occasion turned around out of fear, at the first rock pitch.

After an hour we came to the lower end of the glacier. The next $2^{1/2}$ hours were up that glacier, steeply and sometimes at a 45 degree slope. We passed immense crevasses of breathtaking beauty, like caverns with stalactites and stalagmites of ice, though in the pale pre-dawn light the ice was entirely white. There was no emerald color. The altitude made climbing a challenge. Above a double crevasse, which we crossed on two long aluminum ladders (we were always roped, in case the ice bridge should break, tumbling the ladders into the void), the slope lessened. We stopped for a drink of water. I estimated our altitude at 3,800 meters but Gerd's altimeter registered only 3,640.

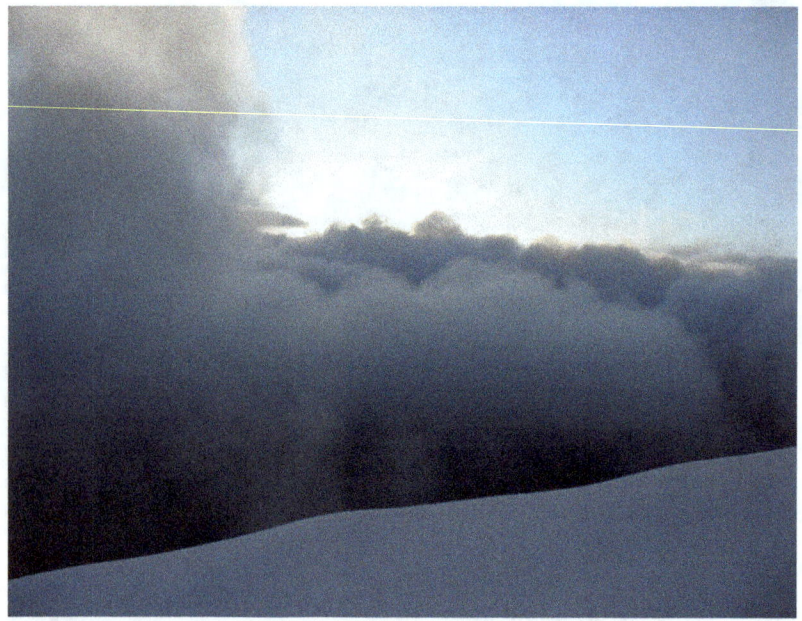

Still nearly a thousand vertical feet to go. I concentrate on my breathing. Two breaths for three steps.

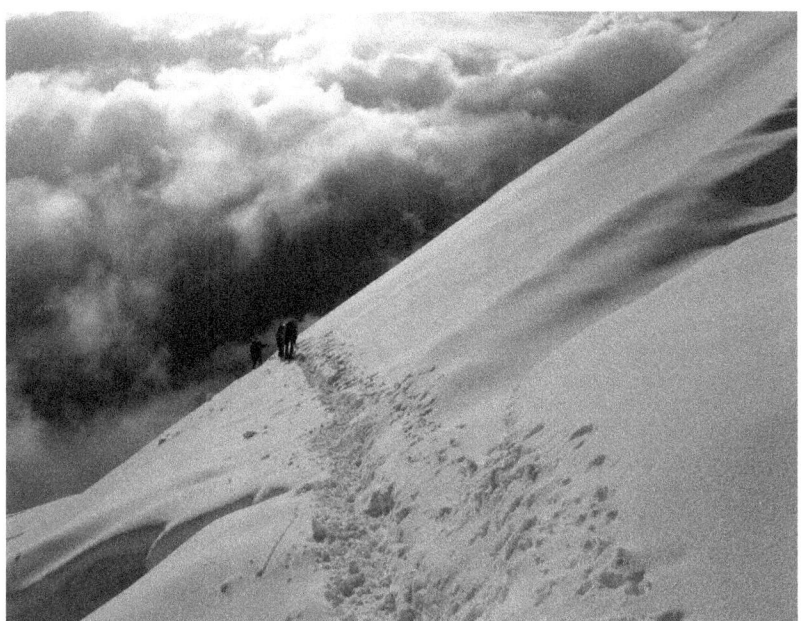

One, two three . . . twenty . . . two, two three . . . twenty. Three hundred sixty breaths for 15 minutes. Finally we were at 3,800 meters, the highest I have ever climbed in Europe. And now the only barrier was the biting wind.

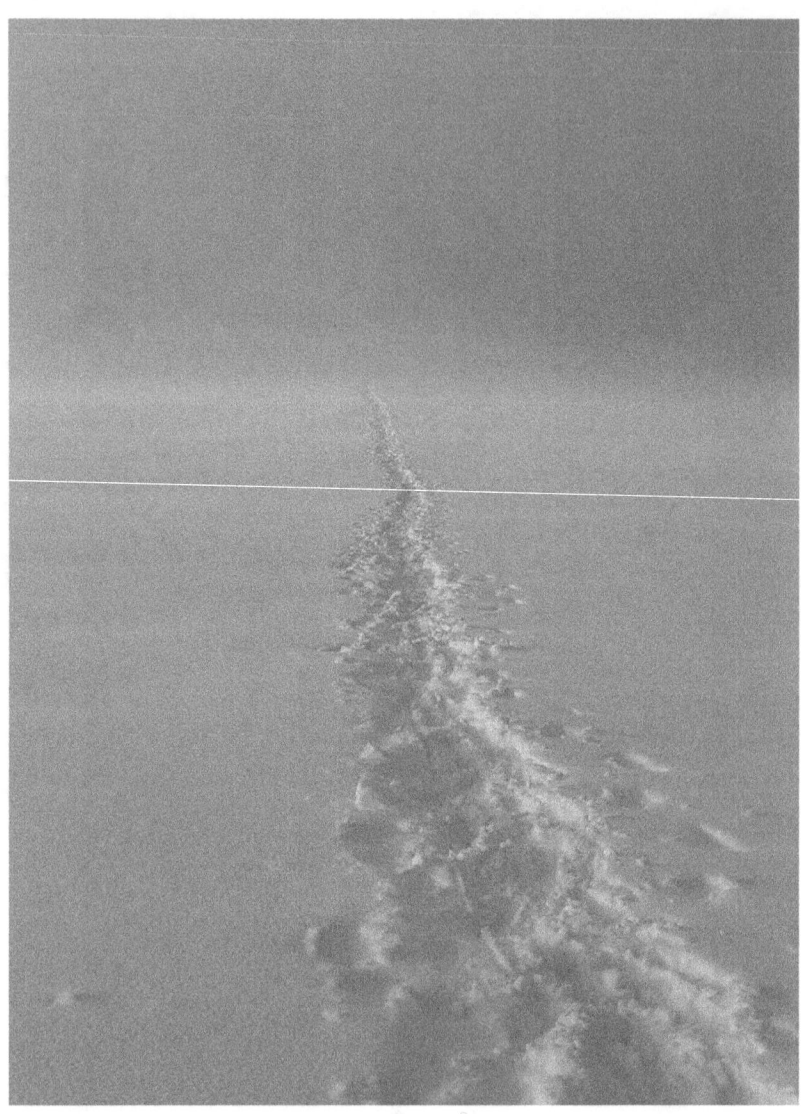

The summit snowfield, half-obscured by wispy cloud, was windblown, cold and icy.

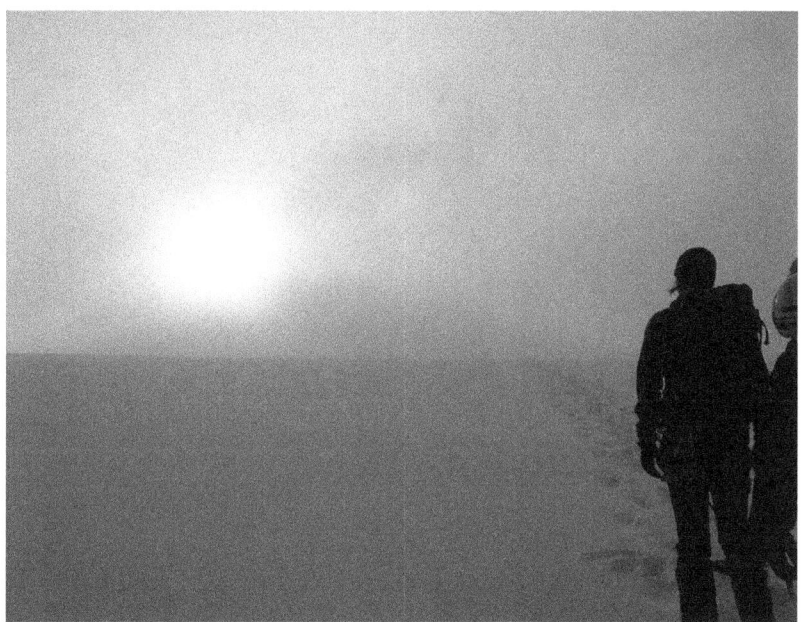

At 8:20 suddenly, the summit cross appeared through the mist that covered the upper slopes.

We are at the summit! 3,905 meters above sea level. One rope is already here and my two tablemates from last night are just arriving up the difficult Hintergrat ridge. Never before, in 50 years of climbing, have I felt such a strong sense that all of us here at the summit have achieved a major climb. This sense of shared accomplishment is entirely new to me. Today is my first major Alpine summit.

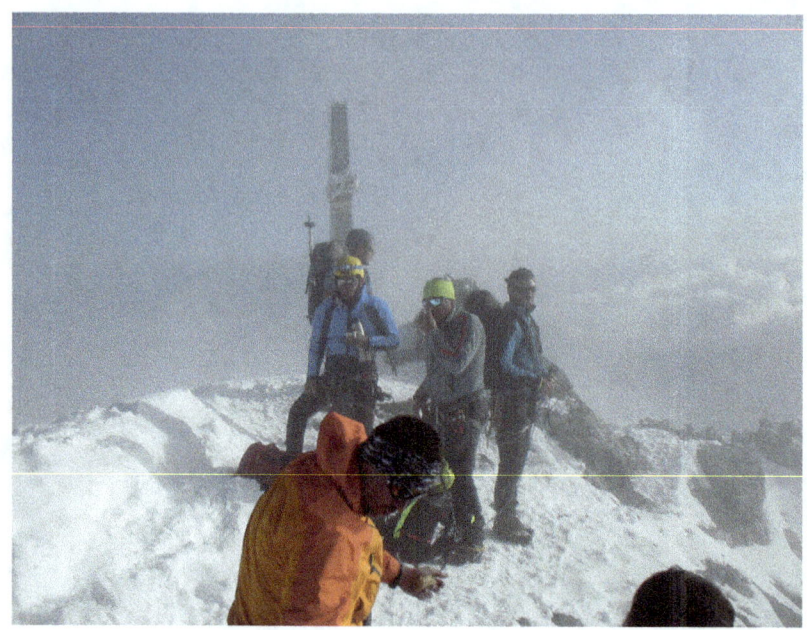

Gerd and I were relatively fast. . . . Gerd says: *"Wenn du schnell am Gipfel kommen willst, musst du langsam gehen."* "If you want to get to the summit quickly, you must go slowly." On the way down, the steep snow-fields are easy and quite fun—no counting of breaths. Climbing on snow is not like walking on a rocky *arête*, which terrifies me to the point that I cannot walk upright for fear of swaying into the abyss. Fear—or fearless-ness—seems to have no logic.

Ascending the final snowfield, Gerd said: "You are in shape; it's all that cross-country skiing." I suppose he is right. I am also aware that I am very lucky. To be able, by whatever means, to keep doing that which gives me such deep pleasure and sense of satisfaction, is a gift and it is precious. I would cross-country ski every day of the winter, to be able to do this for one week in the summer.

We are back at the Payer Hütte at 11 a.m. I will be early for my rendez-vous at the Tabaretta Hut, 2,500 meters elevation. So Gerd and I stop for drinks at Payer. A pleasure to talk with him, friend to friend. Yesterday he promised to accompany me on the hard part down from the hut. Today, that path seems not so narrow as it was on the way up. So we walk and enjoy each other's company. At the end of the *via ferrata*, he stops. He has another client tomorrow for the Ortler, so he will stay at the hut. We embrace, and say good-bye—until next summer.

## Post script:

The hike down to Tabaretta Hut is enjoyable. I go slowly to savor every moment, and I step aside to allow two fellow summiters to go past. The final 800 meters are gentle and I can really relax. I have conquered my fear, at least for this day.

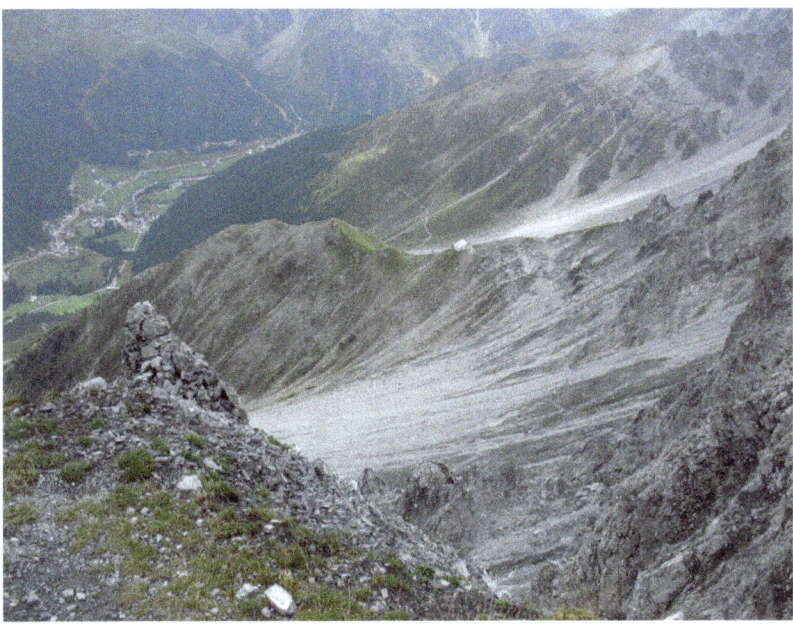

My partner is waiting for me in the restaurant by the picture window that looks out on the trail I have just come along. We order lunch. It has been a long and strenuous climb since breakfast at 4:20. Suddenly there is commotion. People are gesturing towards the window. Up the trail, just where the route becomes quite easy, a group of hikers has gathered. Someone is down, but it is too far to see. A member of the Mountain Rescue Service runs up the trail. A while later, we feel a growing vibration and then a loud drone, as a yellow hospital helicopter arrives, circles, and hovers just above where the crowd has gathered. Two forms descend from the helicopter—emergency medical personnel. Half an hour later, as we are leaving, the helicopter returns. When it takes off again, it flies higher, disappearing over the mountains towards Merano.

A day later, as we are preparing to drive home, we stop in the local supermarket. There is only one other client. It is Gerd! He has hiked down from the Payer Hut after his second ascent of the Ortler in two days, to buy provisions for his third ascent, tomorrow, up the more difficult Hintergrat. Gerd has news about yesterday's emergency—the victim suffered a serious heart attack. More shocking, it was one of the other climbers, on his way down from the summit.

When you climb, you know that an accident is always possible and that even death is a possibility. Two days ago my own fears centered on walking the path between the two huts, precisely where this man collapsed. One thinks (as little as possible, but one does think) of falling. Or of collapsing on the steep climb up in the thin air. But one rarely thinks of collapsing at the bottom of the last difficult section, on the way down.

Erwin Panofsky, the great German art historian, writes of Nicolas Poussin's masterpiece, *Et in Arcadia Ego* (1630, oil on canvas), that even in such a bucolic idyll as this Arcadian pastoral landscape, Death too is present. Yesterday was close to an Arcadian dream for me. Yet, along with the 40 of us who climbed to the summit of the Ortler yesterday, there was one more presence. *Et in Arcadia Ego.*

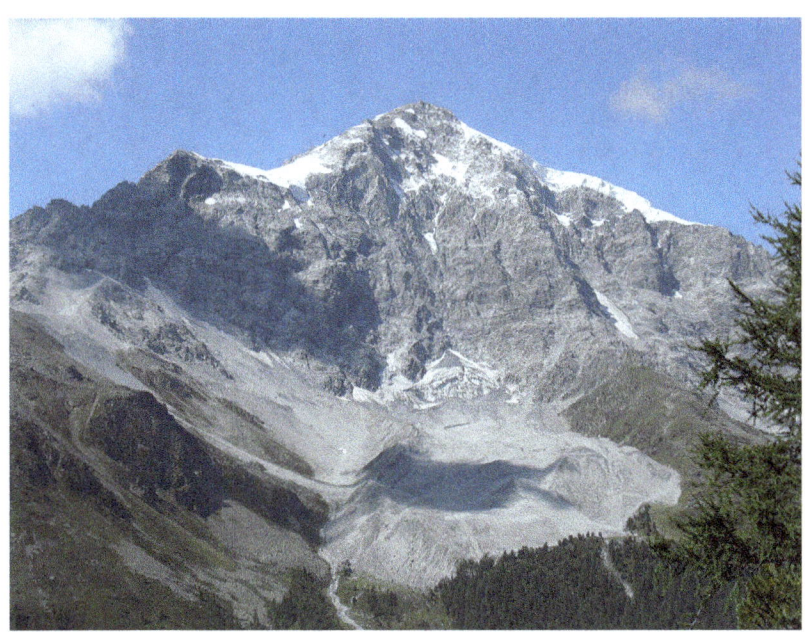

## Images

All photos in this chapter copyright ©Peter Mark 2015

Nicolas Poussin, 1594–1665
*Et in Arcadia Ego, Arcadian Shepherds*, 1630
oil on canvas, 101x82 cm
England, Derbyshire, Chatsworth
Wesleyan University ARTstor ID 40-12-07/ 5
http://library.artstor.org.ezproxy.wesleyan.edu/library/secure/ViewImages?id=
    4jEgcjQrIFhfKi83cVEWRnwkXnMgcA%3D%3D&userId=hzBH&zoomparams=

## ARHA 296: THE MOUNTAINS AND ART HISTORY

*Professor Peter Mark*

## Course Narrative:

This course looks at the important role that mountains have played as artistic inspiration and in the human imagination in Europe and the Americas. From the mountains, humans have drawn both spiritual and artistic inspiration. The course will focus on the Alps, the Black Forest, and the Appalachians.

From the beginnings of civilization, mountains have been associated with the Transcendent. One might say that the first mountain climber in literature was Moses. Early Judaism recognized the mountains as sacred places. In Europe, the earliest recorded climber in the Alps was Ötzi, "the man in the ice," 5,300 years ago.

The Romans built their roads OVER the mountains. This enabled them to avoid building numerous long bridges to span the gorges that cut into mountain valleys. Only later did people look for the low point to bring their goods through the hills. In medieval Europe, passes through and over the Alps and across the ridges of the Black Forest were conduits for the transit of men, of goods, and of cultural forms. Travelers' hostels, associated with religious orders, grew up at the passes, sometimes closely associated with important church architecture. We will track the spread of medieval church frescoes across the Reschen Pass from what is now Italy into present-day Austria and Switzerland. In the nearby Mustairtal, linking Chur (Switzerland) to Südtirol, Charlemagne founded a monastery, the Johanniter Kloster, that still exists. We will study the remains of ninth century frescoes and the magnificent later frescoes (ca. 1200) of the life of John the Baptist.

To look at mountains not as barriers but as passageways, focusing on the links between cultures, is an approach that borrows from Atlantic history. The great Alpine passes have served as paths of cultural exchange for at least 5,000 years. But this role became crucial for artistic development around 1500 A.D. with the movement not only of merchants and trade goods, but also of artists, such as Albrecht Dürer.

The course next traces the increasingly realistic depiction of the Alps by Flemish and Dutch artists. These seventeenth-century painters provide a foretaste of the image of the Alps that is expressed in painting and literature of the Romantic period. The interweaving of the religious and the esthetic with regard to the Alps is already apparent at the end of the 'quattrocento,' in the work of North Italian masters like Giovanni Bellini. Yet it was Netherlandish artists—Bruegel, Seghers, Ruisdael, and especially Joos de Mompers—who, in the sixteenth and seventeenth centuries, first gave full expression to the grandeur, far beyond a human scale, of Alpine scenery.

A crucial change occurred towards the end of the eighteenth century, as the high mountains, which had instilled fear among those who had lived among them and had largely been avoided by travellers, came to be viewed as places of aesthetic beauty and manifestations of the sublime. During the Enlightenment a new scientific spirit of exploration developed. Men began to climb mountains to measure them, just as they measured and classified human beings. This transition led to the birth of mountaineering as a sport.

Romanticism in the visual arts and even more clearly in poetry and in music captures the experience of the Alps as both symbol and physical manifestation of the Transcendent. Constable and Turner depict mountains in England's Lake District and in the Alps as their primary subject matter. A deeper understanding of their landscape painting may be had through the poetry of Wordsworth and Coleridge and the writings of Ruskin. On the continent, Caspar David Friedrich expresses a more solitary sensibility, also deeply informed by the experience of being in the mountains.

In 19th century America, Romantic ideals strongly influence both literature and philosophy—Emerson, Thoreau, Twain. The earliest American landscape painting, the Hudson River School—identified with Cole, Durand, Church—is deeply imbued with both stylistic and thematic elements derived from European Romantic landscapes. Likewise, to appreciate the historical context informing Emersonian Transcendentalism, one needs to be familiar with the writings of Ruskin. For the Hudson River School painters, wilderness and the mountains—whether the Catskills or the Andes—are the embodiment of both the New World and . . . the sublime.

The growth of railroads and the origins of modern tourism ushered in the Age of Mountaineering toward the middle of the nineteenth century. The Alps, and the experience of the sublime, became accessible to the middle classes, themselves a product of the industrial revolution. Narratives of climbing expeditions helped popularize climbing, with major contributions by Leslie Stephen, Edward Whymper, John Tyndall and Mark Twain. We will read selections by these authors.

Mountain photography emerges as an aesthetic medium with the 1907 Italian exploration of the Ruwenzori Mountains, and the images of the Duke of Abruzzi in the same year. We will study these early images. The growing importance of photography is reflected in the images of the postwar British expeditions to Mount Everest (1921, 1922, 1924). Indeed, by 1924 cameras were light enough that George Leigh Mallory had one with him (never found), when he disappeared near the summit of Everest.

In the aftermath of World War I, mountaineering took on a heightened spiritual dimension for men who had survived the horrors of trench warfare. This is demonstrated by Wade Davis in his magisterial study of the British expeditions to Mount Everest between 1921 and 1924 (on our reading list). For the expeditions' sponsors, the effort to climb the world's highest peak was emblematic of the reaffirmation of British imperial power.

The association of mountain climbing with nationalism was even stronger in German-speaking countries. In Austria and Germany, climbing was identified with the cult of physical prowess, and sadly, with ideals of Aryan manliness and with the rise of National Socialism. Anti-Semitism flourished in this context, and the exclusion of Jewish climbers from both the German and the Austrian Alpine Clubs was underway by 1924.

In fact, climbing and skiing in the Alps owed much to Austrian and German Jews and to non-Jewish anti-Nazis. Modern downhill skiing owes more to Hannes Schneider and to Rudolf Gomperz than to any other individuals. Together, they invented the 'genre' of mountain movies. Gomperz was murdered in the Holocaust. Schneider, who fled Austria after 'Anschluss,' helped bring skiing to New England.

In art, too, during the first decades of the twentieth century, mountains were an important source of spiritual inspiration for painters whose work is central to the evolution of modern art. In Cézanne's landscapes, Mont Sainte-Victoire assumes iconic status. Both Nolde and Kirchner drew artistic inspiration from the Swiss Alps. (A close parallel, precisely contemporary, in literature is Thomas Mann's chapter "Schnee," "Snow," in *The Magic Mountain.*) Among Swiss painters, Hodler and Klee create stylistically divergent masterpieces, but both men were inspired by the Alps.

Recently, the extreme-climber-as-photographer shares his vertiginous perch with us. The viewer is left hanging over the void on vertical walls. The practitioners of this art are also writers. The most important of them—including Dave Roberts and Reinhold Messner—are, in fact, better known as climbers and writers than as photographers. For Messner, arguably the greatest high altitude climber of all time, mountains have become the subject of museology. Since retiring from Himalayan climbing, Messner has created five museums in his north Italian home of Südtirol. We conclude the course with a photographic climbing trip to Südtirol.

Readings:

A note on readings: There are two groups of readings for this course. General readings are intended to provide background for the lectures; where possible I have provided a choice of two readings. Most of these selections are art historical monographs. You should read texts *before* the date under which each reading is listed.

Readings marked with an asterisk will serve as the basis for class discussion; again you should read the texts by the date under which they appear (exception: I give you extra time to read Wade Davis). These should be considered core readings.

## Reading list: * recommended for purchase:

Deutscher Alpenverein, *Berg Heil, Alpenverein und Bergsteigen, 1918-1945* (Köln: Böhlau Verlag, 2011).

*Aurel Scheibler Gallery, *Jonathan Bragdon, Tekeningen* (Berlin, 2013).

Ian Bostridge, *Schubert's Winter Journey, Anatomy of an Obsession* (New York: Alfred Knopf, 2015).

Kenneth Clark, *Landscape into Art* (Gibb Press, 2008).

Philip Conisbee and Denis Coutagne, eds., *Cézanne in Provence* (Washington: National Gallery of Art; Aix-en-Provence: Musée Granet; Paris: Réunion des musées nationaux; New Haven: In association with Yale University Press, 2006).

* Wade Davis, *Into the Silence, The Great War, Mallory, and the Conquest of Everest* (New York: Alfred A. Knopf, 2011).

Ralph Waldo Emerson, *Nature and Selected Essays* (Penguin Classics, 2003).

Franz Michael Felder, *Aus Meinem Leben* (Salzburg: Residenz, 1985).

Linda S. Ferber, *Hudson River School: nature and the American vision* (New York: Skira Rizzoli, 2009).

* Patrick Leigh Fermor, *The Broken Road, From the Iron Gates to Mount Athos* (New York: New York Review Books, 2014).

Peter Hanson, *The Summits of Modern Man, Mountaineering after the Enlightenment* (Cambridge: Harvard University Press, 2013).

Heinrich Harrer, *The White Spider: the classic account of the ascent of the Eiger* (New York: J.P. Tarcher/Putnam, 1998).

Jeffrey Hamburger and Susan Marti, eds., *Crown and Veil, Female Monasticism from the Fifth to the Fifteenth Centuries*, (New York: Columbia University Press, 2008).

Agnes Husslein-Arco and Stephan Koja, eds., *Emil Nolde in Radiance and Color* (Chicago: University of Chicago Press, Hirmer Publishers, 2014).

Francis Keenlyside, *Peaks and Pioneers, the Story of Mountaineering* (London: Elek, 1975): Leslie Stephen, "The Ascent of the Schreckhorn," 28-31; "The ascent of the Matterhorn," 37-40.

Joseph Leo Koerner, *Caspar David Friedrich And The Subject Of Landscape* (Reaktion Books, 2009).

Elizabeth Mankin Kornhauser and Amy Ellis, *Hudson River school: masterworks from the Wadsworth Atheneum Museum of Art* (New Haven: Yale University Press in association with the Wadsworth Atheneum Museum of Art, Hartford, 2003).

Hanno Lowe, *Hast Du meine Alpen gesehen? eine jüdische Beziehungsgeschichte.* (Hohenems: Bucher, 2010).

* Thomas Mann, *The Magic Mountain, Der Zauberberg,* trans. H. T. Lowe-Porter (New York: Alfred A. Knopf, 1927, 1977; New York: New Canadian Library, 2014).

Millard Meiss, *Giovanni Bellini's St. Francis in the Frick Collection* (Princeton: Princeton University Press for the Frick Collection, New York, 1964).

Reinhold Messner, *König Ortler* (Lana: Tappeiner; Trento: BQE, 2004).

Roderick Nash, *Wilderness and the American Mind* (New Haven: Yale University Press, 1982).

Thomas Knubben, Tilman Osterwold, Städtische Galerie Altes Theater Ravensburg, *Emil Nolde, Unpainted Pictures, watercolors 1938-1945, from the collection of the Nolde-Stiftung Seebüll.* (Ostfildern-Ruit: Hatje Cantz, 2000).

Earl A. Powell, *Thomas Cole* (New York: Harry A. Abrams, 1990).

David Roberts, *Moments of Doubt, and other mountaineering writings* (Seattle: The Mountaineers, 1986).

Manfred Reuther, Karin Schick, Peter Stamm, *Emil Nolde und die Schweiz* (Köln: DuMont Literatur-u. Kunstverlag; Seebüll, Neukirchen: Nolde Stiftung Seebüll; Davos: Kirchner Museum Davos, 2011).

Adalbert Stifter, *Rock Crystal, Bergkristall,* trans. Marianne Moore, Elizabeth Mayer (New York: New York Review of Books classics, 2008; reprint of edition published: New York: Pantheon Books, 1945).

William H. Truettner and Alan Wallach, eds., *Thomas Cole: landscape into history* (New Haven: Yale University Press; Washington, D.C.: National Museum of American Art, Smithsonian Institution, 1994), 23-77.

* Mark Twain, *A Tramp Abroad* (1880, reprinted: Oxford: Oxford University Press, 1996).

Carel van Tuyll van Serooskerken, and M. Plomp, eds., *Claude Gellée, dit le Lorrain, le dessinateur face à la nature* (Louvre éditions, 2011), 13-36.

Viktoria Von der Brüggen and Christine Peltre, eds., *L'Alsace Pittoresque, L'Invention d'un Paysage* (Unterlinden Museum, 2011).

John B. West, "George I. Finch and his pioneering use of oxygen for climbing at extreme altitudes," *Journal of Applied Physiology*, May 2003, Vol. 94 no. 1702–1713.

William Wordsworth, *The Prelude* in *The Complete Poetical Works* (London: Macmillan and Co., 1888).

## Lecture 1: Introduction to the course

Requirements, expectations, and options
*What do mountains represent to humans?*
    Mountains serve as the embodiment of spiritual power and transcendence
    In a religious context: Symbols of the Transcendent and places of holiness
    In a secular context: Mountains often appear as the embodiment of the sublime
    Aesthetic expression permits the articulation of these feelings through literature
and in the visual arts
* Assignment:
    Write a 1–2 page essay, detailing the reasons for your interest in this course. Include any experience you may have as a mountain hiker or climber. Are you an Art History major? Please tell me which—if any—art history courses you have taken at Wesleyan. If you read German or French, please tell me. The purpose of this essay is to help me to customize the course to you.
    Due: next class session.

## Lecture 2: The socio-economic and cultural implications of mountains

    Mountains and mountain passes as connections, links, paths of communication, rather than as barriers
    The first documented mountain climber Oetzi, the Man in the Ice, 5,200 B.P.
    First iteration: global warming—40 years of glacial melt
    Mountain passes: the Romans and the Via Claudia Augusta

## Lecture 3: Alpine passes and the medieval world

*How did medieval Europe use mountains for protection and for economic gain?*
    The Monastery of St. Johann in Müstair—from Switzerland into Italy
    Charlemagne and the foundation of The Johanniter Kloster
    The ninth century fresco cycle
    The twelfth/thirteenth century fresco cycle
    Gendered religious life in early medieval western Europe
    Monastic life in an Alpine valley; the cloistered Benedictine sisters
    The Abbess as focus of political and economic power

Reading:

Jeffrey Hamburger and Susan Marti, eds., *Crown and Veil, Female Monasticism from the Fifth to the Fifteenth Centuries*, (New York: Columbia University Press, 2008).

## Lecture 4: What impact did the massif of the Alps have on artistic styles?

Secondary centers of mountain-religious art

Taufers—at the junction of north-south and east-west trade routes

Churches as travelers' lodging and refuge

From the notion of high mountain passes to the concept of "pass complex"

the Reschen Complex; carts below, shepherds above.

Medieval monasteries and travellers' refuge;

The Black Forest: Kniebis (1270)

The economic role of pilgrimage

Pilgrimage churches in the mountains

The Church of Allerheiligen (Ottenhöfen)

## Lecture 5: Brief overview of late medieval Italian panel painting.

Alpine Passes and the early medieval world

The Reschenpass—from northern Italy (before it was Italy) into Austria (before it was Austria); the Tirol, south and north, as cultural unit (before it was the Tirol)

Roia/Rojen—the Chapel of St. Nicholas and its 14$^{th}$ century fresco cycle "Germanic" or International style? How terminology shapes our perception

*Five-page paper will be due Week 8

You may select your own theme, but it must be cleared with the professor in advance. Suggested topics:

— Mountains as holy sites

— Archeology of the earliest known Alpinist, Oetzi

— Pilgrimage and the foot traveler (e.g. Santiago de Campostella)

— The Via Claudia Augusta

— The Great St. Bernard Pass

— Artistic representations of hermits and of the wilderness (up to 1650)

## Lecture 6: Renaissance Painting, a broad overview

Artists explore the Natural World, Images of identifiable places, specific peaks

Konrad Witz, Mt. Blanc, 1444

From the generic to the naturalistic; painters depict the mountains, 1300–1550

Late medieval images of mountains as vague or imaginary
Mantua, Palazzo Ducale, ca. 1440, Pisanello
The earliest naturalistic representation of the Alps:
Albrecht Altdorfer; Albrecht Dürer

## Lecture 7: Mood, moment, and place in late fifteenth and sixteenth-century painting Northern Italy

Giovanni Bellini and the Christian discovery of nature
Mountain landscape as mood—the Veneto at sunrise
Renaissance naturalism—Leonardo's landscape drawings
Northern Europe (Flanders and the Netherlands]
Pieter Bruegel as landscape painter
First images of the Bernese Oberland
"Hunters in the Snow" (1565)
Drawn from nature: "View of Walterspurg"

*The first skyscraper?* Bruegel's "The Tower of Babel"
Readings:
Kenneth Clark, *Landscape into Art* (Gibb Press, 2008).
Millard Meiss, *Giovanni Bellini's St. Francis in the Frick Collection* (Princeton: Princeton University Press for the Frick Collection, New York, 1964).

## Lecture 8: Italy: Annibale Carracci and Claude Lorraine; the invention of classical landscape painting

Some Dutchmen in the Alps; From the lowest to the highest point in Europe;
Herkules Seghers, Joos de Momper, Jacob von Rusidael
Reading:
Carel van Tuyll van Serooskerken, and M. Plomp, eds., *Claude Gellée, dit le Lorrain, le dessinateur face à la nature* (Louvre éditions, 2011), 13-36. (If you do not read French, just enjoy the images.)

## Lecture 9: The Enlightenment and early scientific interest in the Alps; Taming of the wilderness; from hunting parties to the first mountain guides

The Enlightenment and the origins of Mountaineering
de Saussure and Mont Blanc
The pastoral and the picturesque: painting the Vosges mountains in France

Reading:

* Peter Hanson, *The Summits of Modern Man, Mountaineering after the Enlightenment* (Cambridge: Harvard University Press, 2013), chapter 1, chapter 2.

Optional Reading: Viktoria Von der Brüggen and C. Peltre, eds., *L'Alsace Pittoresque, L'Invention d'un Paysage* (Unterlinden Museum, 2011).

## Lecture 10: Romanticism

A broad literary, musical and artistic movement, Romanticism was the dominant cultural orientation in early nineteenth century Europe; it is most closely identified with German writers (Heine, Goethe), artists, musicians, and philosophers. We will read English Romantic poetry, Wordsworth's *The Prelude*.

Caspar David Friedrich, and the art of German Romanticism

Dawn and twilight and the evocation of mood

The Bavarian mountains

Winter snow and graveyards

Readings:

Joseph Leo Koerner, *Caspar David Friedrich and The Subject Of Landscape* (Reaktion Books, 2009).

Ian Bostridge, *Schubert's Winter Journey, Anatomy of an Obsession* (New York: Alfred Knopf, 2015).

Listening:

Franz Schubert "Winterreise."

## Lecture 11: How sublime was life in the mountains?

*Farm Life in an Alpine Valley in nineteenth century Austria: Did artists distort the reality of life in the Alps?*

Franz Michael Felder (1839-1869)—the extraordinary autobiography of a self-educated farmer

"My life is a mirror of our condition;" the narrow social world of the Bregenzerwald

Felder's autobiography, *Aus meinem Leben*, was first published by his children in 1904. It has never been translated into English. If you read German, this is A MUST-READ for this course.

Visual Images of Alpine Village Life:

Romanticizing the Rustic; or, "They should have read Felder"

"Peasants of Chamoni," 1823

M. Villeneuve, "Lettres sur la Suisse," 1823-1832

The guides: Valtornanche, 1867

Readings:

Franz Michael Felder, *Aus Meinem Leben* (Salzburg: Residenz, 1985).

(I shall provide you with translations of selected passages.)

*Adalbert Stifter, *Rock Crystal, Bergkristall,* trans. Marianne Moore, Elizabeth Mayer
    (New York: New York Review of Books classics, 2008; reprint of edition published:
    New York: Pantheon Books, 1945).

## Lecture 12: Guest Lecture: English Romanticism; Emeritus Professor Alfred Turco

Reading:

* William Wordsworth, *The Complete Poetical Works* (London: Macmillan and Co.,
    1888), Selections from *The Prelude*.

Guest Lecture to be followed by: The English landscape painters: John Constable and
    J.M.W. Turner.

## Extra lecture: Guest Speaker: Stephen Belcher, independent scholar

"Two Yankee Artists in the Green Mountains: Martha Wood Belcher (1844-1930) and
    Hilda Belcher (1880-1963)"

## Lecture 13: Wilderness and the American Mind

Thomas Cole, Asher B. Durand and The Hudson River School
Frederic Church (of Hartford)

## Class Field trip: Wadsworth Atheneum Museum of Art, Hartford, Connecticut

Wilderness as a definitive characteristic of the new nation; the Catskill Mountains as
respite from urban life; Frederic Church and Manifest Destiny.

Transcendentalism, Ralph Waldo Emerson

Reading:

*Ralph Waldo Emerson, *Nature and Selected Essays* (Penguin Classics, 2003), Intro-
    duction and "Nature." Or, online: http://www.emersoncentral.com/nature.htm

Also, read one of the following:

Earl A. Powell, *Thomas Cole* (New York: Harry A. Abrams, 1990).

William H. Truettner and Alan Wallach, eds., *Thomas Cole: landscape into history*
    (New Haven: Yale University Press; Washington, D.C.: National Museum of
    American Art, Smithsonian Institution, 1994), 23-77.

Roderick Nash, *Wilderness and the American Mind* (New Haven: Yale University Press, 1982).

## Lecture 14: Hudson River School

German connections: the Düsseldorf School of landscape painting
The second generation: John Kensett, Sanford Gifford, Robert Duncanson, Church's later work, Albert Bierstadt
Reading: ONE of the following:
Linda S. Ferber, *Hudson River School: nature and the American vision* (New York: Skira Rizzoli, 2009).
Elizabeth Mankin Kornhauser and Amy Ellis, *Hudson River School: Masterworks from the Wadsworth Atheneum Museum of Art* (New Haven: Yale University Press in association with Wadsworth Atheneum Museum of Art, Hartford, 2003).

## Lecture 15: Bringing the Sublime to Europe's leisured class

Mountain climbing as metaphor for religious experience; the artistic expression of the Sublime in literature and in art
Mountain climbing, mountain literature, and the Transcendent
A sport for 'literati:' the playground of Europe
Edward Whymper, Sir Leslie Stephen, Mark Twain
The romance of death: the mystique of climbing accidents
July 14, 1865—Matterhorn first ascent; the day the rope broke
The artistic representation of mortality in the mountains
Mark Twain—laughing past the graveyard
Readings:
Francis Keenlyside, *Peaks and Pioneers, the Story of Mountaineering* (London: Elek, 1975): Leslie Stephen, "The Ascent of the Schreckhorn," 28-31; "The ascent of the Matterhorn," 37-40.
* Mark Twain, *A Tramp Abroad* (1880, reprinted: Oxford: Oxford University Press, 1996), chapters xxii; xxiii; xxviii, xxix, chapter xxxiii xxxiv, xxxv, through xxxviii, and xxxix-xli.
Thomas Mann, *The Magic Mountain, Der Zauberberg*, trans. H. T. Lowe-Porter (New York: Alfred A. Knopf, 1927, 1977; New York: New Canadian Library, 2014), the chapter entitled "Snow."

## * REQUIRED field trip to New York City

We will visit the Metropolitan Museum of Art and the Frick Collection

Lecture 16: The Alps as musical inspiration: Did this differ from the response of painters?

Late Romanticism—the Alps as symphonic inspiration
    Richard Strauss, "An Alpine Symphony," and Gustav Mahler, Symphony no. 3.
    Early mountain photography—from the Duke of Abruzzi
The growth of broad-based tourism
Reading:
* Wade Davis, *Into the Silence, The Great War, Mallory, and the Conquest of Everest*
    (New York: Alfred A. Knopf, 2011). Begin reading .

Lecture 17: German Expressionism

*How did early twentieth century painters express both the intimate and the infinite?*
    Emil Nolde and the Swiss Alps
    From Emil Hansen, mountain climber and drawing professor, to postcard designer
and watercolorist Emil Nolde
    Spontaneity: capturing the moment and mood of the high mountains
    'Die Brücke': Karl Schmidt-Rottluff and Ernst Ludwig Kirchner
Reading: ONE of the following:
Thomas Knubben, Tilman Osterwold, Städtische Galerie Altes Theater Ravensburg,
    *Emil Nolde, Unpainted Pictures, watercolors 1938-1945, from the collection of the
    Nolde-Stiftung Seebüll* (Ostfildern-Ruit: Hatje Cantz, 2000).
Agnes Husslein-Arco and Stephan Koja, eds., *Emil Nolde in Radiance and Color* (Chi-
    cago: University of Chicago Press, Hirmer Publishers, 2014).
Manfred Reuther, Karin Schick, Peter Stamm, *Emil Nolde und die Schweiz* (Köln:
    DuMont Literatur-u. Kunstverlag; Seebüll, Neukirchen: Nolde Stiftung Seebüll;
    Davos: Kirchner Museum Davos, 2011). (for German speakers)

Lecture 18: The sublime, death and transfiguration: 1914-2014, World War I and its aftermath

*Did war lend a new spiritual meaning to the mountains?*
    English and German mountain memorials to the dead
    George Leigh Mallory, Empire, and the romance of Everest
Reading:
* Wade Davis, *Into the Silence, The Great War, Mallory, and the Conquest of Everest*
    (New York: Alfred A. Knopf, 2011), especially 1-124.

## Lecture 19: Between the wars, 1919-1939

*How did political ideologies capture the Alps?*

Nationalism, the Alpine Clubs (Alpenvereine) and the appropriation of mountaineering by National Socialism

The first ski schools—Hannes Schneider and St. Anton, Vorarlberg

The Eiger Nordwand, 1936–1938; the first ascent and Nazi propaganda

The German and Austrian Alpine Clubs and the exclusion of Jewish members

Reading:

John B. West, "George I. Finch and his pioneering use of oxygen for climbing at extreme altitudes," *Journal of Applied Physiology*, May 2003, Vol. 94 no. 1702-1713. Or online: http://jap.physiology.org/content/94/5/1702

Optional readings:

Heinrich Harrer, *The White Spider: the classic account of the ascent of the Eiger* (New York: J.P. Tarcher/Putnam, 1998).

Berg Heil, *Alpenverein und Bergsteigen, 1918-1945* (Köln: Böhlau Verlag, 2011).


## Lecture 20: Early twentieth-century Modernist painting and the Alps

Switzerland: Ferdinand Hodler and Paul Klee

Paul Cézanne and Mont Sainte-Victoire—the iconic mountain of modernism


Reading:

Philip Conisbee and Denis Coutagne, eds., *Cézanne in Provence* (Washington: National Gallery of Art; Aix-en-Provence: Musée Granet; Paris: Réunion des musées nationaux; New Haven: In association with Yale University Press, 2006).


## *Lecture 21: Visit to Davison Art Center

Recent Mountain Photography and Travel Writing

Technological innovation—lighter cameras and lighter climbing equipment—and the challenge of photographing the moment while climbing.

Reading:

*Patrick Leigh Fermor, *The Broken Road, From the Iron Gates to Mount Athos* (New York: New York Review Books, 2014), 284-290.

Looking:

Study the illustrations in one of the following works (NOT only for German-speakers):

Reinhold Messner, *König Ortler* (Lana: Tappeiner; Trento: BQE, 2004); or

David Roberts, *Moments of Doubt, and other mountaineering writings* (Seattle: The Mountaineers, 1986).

## Lecture 22: Jewish presence in the Alps

The *Bergfilm*—Arnold Fanck and Gomperz, inventors of the ski movie

Film segments: *Der Heilige Berg*, (1926); *Der weisse Rauch* (1931); *Der Wolken-phänomene von Malaga*, (1924)

Hannes Schneider and the invention of Alpine skiing, 1910-1931

Exile or Auschwitz—divergent destinies: Schneider; Fanck, and Gomperz

Reading:

Hanno Lowe, *Hast Du meine Alpen gesehen* (Hohenems: Bucher, 2010). This exhibition catalog, unfortunately not available in English, is a history of the Jewish presence in the Alps.

## Lecture 23: Contemporary mountain landscape drawing

The philosopher as artist—creating a universe; chronicling the Dent du Midi (mountain in Switzerland near Lake Geneva)

The art of Jonathan Bragdon

Readings:

* Galerie Aurel Scheibler, *Jonathan Bragdon, Tekeningen* (Berlin: Aurel Scheibler, 2013), especially the essays by Block and Meyer-Krahmer.

Conclusions and Summary

*Final research paper (10 pages) due at the end of Reading Period

## ACKNOWLEDGEMENTS

As senior editor, I acknowledge and thank my hard-working and immensely talented co-editors, Penny Snyder (Wesleyan 2016) and Peter Helman (Wesleyan 2015). Peter and Penny shared equally with me the task of selecting and then editing the manuscripts. I wish to thank and congratulate them, along with the other student authors, for the clarity, the originality, and the style of their contributions. That undergraduates should write so well is a tribute to them . . . and to their university. For this book is truly a Wesleyan University project, and its publication reflects both institutional and individual support. Here, I thank a few of the many who have played a role in *The Mountains in Art History*.

First, to my colleagues in Art History, who encouraged me, their Africanist, to "teach my passion," I offer my heartfelt thanks. Second, to all of my students in the three iterations of "ARHA 296": thank you for challenging me, for sharing your own enthusiasm for the high hills, and—the idea was yours—for suggesting that we consider writing our own text for the course.

Special gratitude is due to my colleague Andrew Curran. During his term as Dean of the Humanities, Andy encouraged me to teach the course, worked with me to arrange field trips, helped me to apply for crucial grant support, and encouraged us when the book seemed only a fantasy.

To the Allbritton Center for the Study of Public Life, for a grant enabling me to take students on a research trip to the archives of the

Appalachian Mountain Club in Boston (and to the AMC staff for welcoming our visit).

To the Wesleyan administration for a grant to employ my co-editors as student interns.

To Dean Curran's successor, Ellen Nerenberg, and to Joyce Jacobson (vice president for Academic Affairs) for arranging the funding to publish this book both online and in a digital version.

To Suzanna Tamminen, director of Wesleyan University Press, for daring to take on this student-written book. . . . When I reread the essays, I understand that this was not so much a dare as recognition of the intellectual quality of the essays.

To Victoria Stahl for her friendly and tireless copy editing, for tracking down incomplete references, and for correcting errors that slipped by the three editors.

To Professor *Emeritus* Alfred Turco for guiding me through the English Romantic literature that has become a crucial element in the course and in this book.

To my guide, Gerd Schönthaler, whose expertise got me up the Ortler and whose friendship has brightened my Alpine climbing for the past five years.

To the counselors at North Country Camps, where my own passion for the mountains was born, and especially to Pete Gucker, long-time Director of Camp Lincoln and long-time friend.

On the day in 2013 that I received the enrollment list for my new course on the mountains, one name stood out: "Peter Mark Helman." I wrote to him to say that this was the first time I would have myself as a student. Little did we suspect: as a student and as a co-author and as co-editor. To Peter Helman and to Penny Snyder, I express my deepest gratitude.

Strasbourg, France
June 24, 2016